The Ring of Chairs

a Medium's Story
of her training by Spirit Guides

by
Janet Cyford

a traditional
British Spiritualist Medium

A sane and sensible approach to
Spiritual Unfoldment and the Development of Mediumship
in the Home Circle

First published in 2000 by
Thirteen ~O~Seven Press
1307 Argonne Drive
Baltimore, Maryland 21218

ISBN 0-9678296-0-7

www.HomeCircles.com

JCMedsp@aol.com

Printed in the United States of America by
BCP Digital Printing
Baltimore, Maryland 21215

Cover Design by Janet Cyford
Graphics by Gabriel Galluccio
Art Work and layout by Michelle Pierlussi

Dedicated to my dear husband Al Cyford,
my daughter Angela and my son David.
Also to my family, friends and coworkers here
. . . and in the hereafter.

To
Howard
with love + friendship
Janet Cyford
Jan. 2004.

"Your thoughts are Living Things, use them wisely."

Janet Cyford

Introduction

There have always been individuals, who possess a natural ability to see and talk with those, who have passed through the transition we call death. Spiritual gifts of inner sight had special meaning in ancient times. Young *sensitives* who displayed these abilities, received nurturing and protection to shield them from the harshness of life in the outside world. Within the confines of a temple, they learned to govern their personality with self-discipline, in order to become clear vessels for Spiritual Healing or to carry the word of the Great Spirit.

Special attention to strengthening the nervous system of the sensitive, prevented undue strain and impairment. Communication with the world of Spirit has always been a fragile process dependant upon harmonious conditions. Its delicate balance is easily disturbed, so every effort to prevent discord, helped to achieve successful contact between the two realities.

When organised religion took on the responsibility for spiritual interpretation, people willingly believed, what their religious advisers told them to believe. The church promised eternal life to all who obeyed the rules, and eternal damnation to anyone whose differing opinions, threatened their power. It became impossible for, sensitive's with inner sight, to speak of all they knew to be true. For now they were shunned, as outcasts and heretics. A danger to the church's power, they had to be stopped from leading the masses to think and reason for themselves. Many sensitive souls suffered greatly at the hands of their persecutors. Believing God no longer performed miracles, the church saw this phenomena as the work of the devil.

Hundreds lost their lives for admitting they heard voices or saw visions. Some suffered physical torture, until they denied their truth. Many died by fire at the stake, others were buried alive. There is a small country town in England, whose local pond was the scene for *ducking* these offenders. The victims' only crime, was to speak of their awareness of another reality. The clergy accused them of using dark powers, for the church controlled the masses with fear and superstition.

In Great Britain, in 1937, a committee of Anglicans, appointed by the Archbishops of Canterbury and York, investigated Spiritualism, the possibility of Spirit communication and the claims of Spiritualists. After two years careful study, the committee submitted its reports, to the House of Bishops. Their reply was eagerly awaited by the committee and the general public. Up until then, the Church of England had given no guidance to the rank and file regarding the possiblity of Spirit communication.

The committees findings were never available for the general public and soon it was learned, the House of Bishops had buried its contents. The reports were kept secret for nine years, when a copy of the Majority Report, mysteriously appeared on the desk of A. W. Austen. After verifying the document's authenticity, it was printed in its entirety in the Spiritualist newspaper, "Psychic News." Copies of "The Church of England and Spiritualism," are still available and can be obtained from the Spiritualist National Union.

People who will not reason for themselves have difficulty accepting that, which shakes their unbending sense of reality. By continuing to distrust and dismiss the claims of the sensitive who *sees* with inner sight, we foster the superstitions of the ignorant and ill-informed. There are many who still choose to dismiss this phenomena, of communication between the two realities, as the work of the devil.

Many believe in the continuing existence of the Soul beyond this earthly life. Some have found proof, convincing them of the existence of an afterlife. Those who have the ability to communicate directly with the Spirit World, will find the following informative. Under Spirit's directive, it is designed to educate in the subtleties and mechanics of Modern Mediumship, and Spirit communication.

The uninformed, who accept the media's portrayal of Spirit communication via a Medium will, it is hoped, learn something new. Mediums no longer receive Spirit messages, tapped in knocks and raps. This type of Physical phenomena requires ectoplasm and a physical Medium, rarities in the present day.

There are many on the earth today who have overcome the personality with their Soul's inner knowledge. They respond to the spiritual energy bathing the earthplane by raising their consciousness, allowing the inherent Divinity within, to outwardly manifest in their lives.This book centres on the author's personal experience as a Spiritualist Medium. The development of Mental Mediumship and the essential cooperation with Spirit Guides. Seeking Self Mastery, Soul growth and Soul culture.

From the Author

My reasoning, and justification for writing this book began sometime ago. Disheartened by the lack of good Mediumship and offended by the media's promotion of psychism, I decided to share what I had learned of Spirit communication. I thought it was my idea to do so but found, some way into my writing, it was not my idea at all. Spirit had sown the seed and bowing to their wisdom, and cooperating with their suggestions, the chapters flowed with unexpected ideas. As is often the case when we attempt a project Spirit intercedes, steering us to circumstances that reinforce or re-educate our beliefs.

The tenets, taught to me regarding life after death in the Spirit realms, were extremely simple. The existence of the Soul is continuous, there is no death other than that of the material body. All that we are, continues, to be. The Soul, Spiritual Self, consciousness and character prevail. All that died was the outworn overcoat. What is buried or cremated was the temporary vehicle used for our earthly visit. But more than this was shown to me, for not only did the Soul survive, but, physical death did not sever the links of love and friendship that bind us together. The world of Spirit, to which the Soul returns, is intimately involved with our material reality. It does not exist in some far away location, but merely vibrates on a different frequency than the one we have become accustomed to.

From early childhood I had watched my aunt and my father, slip with ease into a state of trance, allowing one of many Guides to speak through them. They did not step into the physical body, as some believe, but spoke to us by blending with the Medium's physical organs of speech and hearing. All this depended on loving cooperation, between the Medium in this earthly reality and the Guide in the Spirit reality. This quality of Deep Trance Mediumship is now rare and sorely missed.

What passes for communication from Spirit today, is poor in performance, content and delivery and lacks the dignity and ease of the genuine phenomena of yesteryear. Every aspect of Modern

Mediumship is now placed under the umbrella of *Channeling*. It does not matter what we call ourselves. However, it matters when simple spiritual truths, taught by Spirit Guides are adulterated with weird and strange beliefs.

My experiences and conclusions will definitely offend those ingrained in the tenets of their own sacred cows. I make no apology for this. Inspired and encouraged by my colleagues in Spirit, I speak and teach from my own lifetime experience of the reality of the afterlife and the continuing contact taking place for those of us with the natural ability to recognise the presence of a Spirit communicator.

The bedrock of all Mediumship is the Development Circle. Spiritual unfoldment and Soul culture must accompany this type of development which can only be achieved in the safety of a well-run circle group. Therefore, the core of this book deals with the formation of such groups and the imagined obstacles preventing people forming a group without a practicing Medium.

It is a sane and simple approach to a much maligned and misunderstood, misrepresented and ridiculed subject. It will teach something new to all who read these pages. In its delivery I have satisfied my need to pass on to others that, which I know to be true.

Table of Contents

The Family Circle 1

Members of my family left London to avoid the constant bombing raids. They chose to evacuate to Ilfracombe, a small seaside town on the West Coast of England. Spirit contact begins with a family member, during the Second World War in London, England.

Mediumship and the Medium 3

A Medium's training takes place on all levels. Body, Mind and Spirit. There are still many misconceptions about the ability to speak with those in Spirit A great deal is expected of the potential Medium . . . Self-discipline and self-mastery. Governing the sensitivity is essential. Communication is governed by Spiritual Laws that come into effect when a Medium reaches for a link with Spirit. Having the gift of Mediumship does not bestow instant spirituality, humility or honesty, these qualities must be cultivated. Mental imagery received by the Medium is created in thought by the Spirit contact.

Carrying On 7

From the top of the stairs, I saw my father lying in the hallway below. Overcome with curiosity, he lay listening at the door of the seance room. Turning to find me standing above him, he motioned me to be quiet and beckoned me down to join him. The close contact my father developed with his Chinese Guide, was evident in the change of his features whenever the Oriental was near. My presence in the home *circle* during the war, must have been for my safety. Although this, was never given as the reason.

Deep Trance Mediumship 9

The development of trance Mediumship needs suitable group members, and cooperation in both realities, for this to be successful. A Spirit Guide uses the physical apparatus of the unconscious personality, rather than the attuned mind of the conscious clairvoyant. It is still a blending of energies, not as some believe, Spirit possession.

Early Beginnings.. 13

How rare the gift of true Mediumship is . . . Its purpose . . . Cooperation with Spirit teachers and dedication to the process of development. "There is no death," was the message Spirit communicators wanted to impress upon us. Anxious to let their families know they were well, loved ones in Spirit gave verifiable evidence via the Medium. Modern Spiritualist movement sprang from the humble beginnings of the Fox sisters' experiences in New York State. Widespread interest swept across America and Great Britain. Spiritualism was formed as a religion, to protect its Mediums and Healers from persecution and imprisonment.

How do people cope with the loss of a loved one without this understanding? What continues to exist after the physical body dies? The injustices we do when rehashing the gruesome details of a person's death. Fear of dying adds to our dread of growing old. In thought, we create our own reality, through religious dogma, many live in fear of what is beyond.

Through the deep trance Mediumship of my aunt, Spirit promised our safety. With the utmost trust in their promise the circle members met regularly throughout the war years even if there was an air raid! We survived those dangerous times and were saved from harm, in the relentless bombing raids. Spirit intervened again sometime before Nan had a close call with death.

They talked of the reality of life after death; and how intimately involved, the Spirit world is with our material one. One of my favourite subjects was conception! When did the Soul enter the physical shell? Was it at conception, quickening, or at the time of birth?

The origin of these principles, given by Spirit through the Mediumship of Emma Hardinge Britten, an American Medium.

1. The Fatherhood of God

Teachers from the world of Spirit, never define God as an authoritative figure dispensing reward or punishment, nor do they personify this energy of goodness.

2. The Brotherhood of Man

This is a brotherhood of humankind not of gender. It is a spiritual law that recognizes each human as being part of one another, irrespective of colour, race or creed.

3. The Communion of Spirits and the Ministry of Angels

We are assisted at all times by a vast multitude of Souls in Spirit. Some assistance comes from higher levels of Soul existence where our sincere prayers are responded to by beings who have passed beyond the confines of personality and ego. Our personal communion with this world of Spirit is a natural phenomena.

4. The Continuous Existence of the Human Soul

Soul progression is open to everyone and the greater 'Self' acknowledges its own mortality. On an intuitive level we know we have been, we are, and we shall always be. Ties of love transcend all levels of being and death does not sever these ties.

5. Personal Responsibility

Under spiritual law we are accountable for our thoughts, words and deeds. When the earthly personality takes personal responsibility for that, which it alone has put into motion, a great inner alignment forms. Along with an acceptance of this principle comes the understanding that human beings alone are responsible for the suffering experienced in this material life.

6. Compensation & Retribution for all good & evil deeds done on earth

The great spiritual law of cause and effect is escaped by no one. Our thoughts, words and deeds follow us, until such time that the scales of compensation or retribution are balanced through love. This is the responsibility inherent in the gift of free will and the law is perfect.

7. Eternal Progress open to every Soul

In the eyes of Spirit, the accomplishments of the Soul are only learned through experience. On its pathway back to the Godforce, the Soul must use its free will to fashion the Soul into a vehicle for the true expression of the spiritual self. Eternal progress fulfills our earthly law of human rights. No sin is so great that a Soul is denied progression, but it must seek this for itself. No other can redeem us, neither can we be absolved for our own actions. Our motive measures the seriousness of personal transgression and through the law of love we can make amends.

vii

an emotional initiation, when the inner spiritual self tells us *"you will survive."* Spiritual teachers who walked this earth plane.

Ancient wisdom from ancient cultures. The ease of Spirit contact in China.

North American Indians and the warriorship of the Soul. Geometric shapes reveal an Egyptian influence. Information comes in other ways. With synchronicity? No, with Spirit orchestration.

Guides have played an important part in my life. Through chance conversation with strangers, I have been led to people whose spiritual gifts enhanced my life. One of these connections brought me into the Spirit presence of a Blackfoot Indian, who became my greatest teacher.

My Grandmother, Nan returns to tell us,"One of the babies is a girl." Guidance as the twins grew in safety, watched over by their own Guides. David and his whistling grandmother.

Joining a group for Mediumistic development in my late twenties. The Greek aspect of Atheon. A love for allegory and symbolism. First public lecture. Stage fright has never left me, although it is now easier to govern.

Spirit Guides have often forewarned me of difficulties ahead. Never with specific detail, but with words of wisdom that prepared me in advance. My father gives a birth date.

My Spirit colleagues have never asked or expected me to lay aside, my free will. They taught me it is God's gift to humankind. Our purpose is to exercise our free will, until we can voluntarily surrender it to the will of God. We can a willingly work with Spirit, or experience our lives, in a different ways. Personal experiences taught me to protect the awareness, shielding it from extraneous thoughts and the influence of occult powers.

The partnership every Medium wishes for . . . Foreseen by my aunt on the last occasion we were together. A transatlantic courtship and romance. The power of Spirit brings two people together.

experience of this spark of Divinity is sought by many Souls inhabiting the earth plane today.

Members of a development group, sit in a circle of chairs in the seance room. Circle group work, is the foundation upon which Spiritual Unfoldment and Mediumship stand. The purpose of Mediumship and Spirit contact. True Mediumship cannot be developed alone, nor learned by attending lectures or reading do-it-yourself books. Many potentially gifted Mediums are content with little training and settle for fortune telling. A renewed interest in sitting r for further development, in the safety of the group circle, would educate and raise the standard of Mediumship beyond the New Age fringe of psychic channellers. Mediumship is not for the unsteady of mind or the overblown ego.

Practical advice for forming a group for Spiritual Unfoldment and Mediumistic Development. The most important component, the group leader. Aims and Intentions of the group. Centering in the Spiritual Self. Prayer to open the awareness. Healing exercises, personal and Absent Healing. Healing groups Expanding the Consciousness. Conscious Journeying. All in the Telling. Preparing New Groupies. Clairvoyance, The Art of "Seeing." clairvoyantly. Closing and Protecting the Sensitivity.

Determining the suitability of a new student . . . Their motives for seeking this type of unfoldment. Can they follow directions from the group leader are they willing too. Regular attendance, commitment to their personal development. This work is nondenominational . . . Spirit teaching embraces all faiths. The Psychic who tells fortunes has difficulties fitting into this type of discipline . . . So does the one who believes they have a special mission. The talkative wordy student . . . respecting a rule of confidentiality. Difficult conditions for Spirit to work in . . . when atmosphere is heavy with criticism.

Finding a sensible method of development. Without like-minded companions for support, it can be dangerous. The Law of Attraction draws others to us. Ask God for help. Seek Spirit guidance, Soul and spiritual unfoldment along with Mediumistic development. Avoid cluttering the mind with various psychic subjects, the individual who specializes develops quicker than the one spread too thinly over many subjects. Learn to 'know thyself' and take personal responsibility for all of your actions. An abuse of drugs or alcohol damages the protective web and addicts are excluded from this development.

Glossary

A guide to the meaning inherent within the phraseology used by the Author.

Afterlife, (The)

The reality the Soul, Spiritual Self and our full consciousness will return to, at the moment of physical death. (See Spirit World)

Attunement

To bring into a harmonious or responsive relationship. An alignment and rapport with another.

Aura

The energy emanating from anything that holds a spark of the Divine.

Clairsentience

Clear sensing. A blending of all the extended senses. Without vision or sound.

Clairvoyance

Clear Seeing. A natural ability of the Soul to receive visions, signs and symbols. At the time of writing its meaning has been distorted to, the ability to predict the future.

Clairvoyant, (A)

One who uses inner sight.

Consciousness

Awareness, perception . . . that which is cognizant.

Cooperation

An active and willing participation in a harmonious, collaborative effort.

Deep Trance Mediumship

Communication with Spirit through the means of deep trance. Not to be confused with modern day "channelling."

Emotional Self

That which is formed by our destructive or constructive emotional reactions to events in our lives.

Energy Field

The energy surrounding all that holds a Spark of the Divine. That which expands when the consciousness is raised. (See Aura)

Evidence of Soul Survival

Verifiable information that proves the continuation of life after death.

Field of sensitivity

An extended, altered state of awareness, which senses, perceives and registers the energy presence of another.

Greater Self, (The)

The totality of ones being, including that not yet manifested or recognised.

Inner strength

The core of strength found within the Spiritual Self.

Materialism

Concern with only that, which is impermanent and transitory.

Medium, (A)

The vehicle or instrument through which Spirit contact is achieved.

Medium, Spiritualist (A)

A Spirit trained Medium. One who demonstrates the tenants of Spiritualism through their Mediumship.

Mediumship

The self-mastery to use one's psychic ability to register the presence of a Spirit communicator or Spirit companion and to work in cooperation with that reality.

Metaphysical

Theoretical, vague, speculative, and unsubstantial. Communication with Spirit is not based on speculative or abstract reasoning, neither is it theoretical.

Metaphysics

Speculation upon questions that are unanswerable to scientific observation, analysis, or experiment. Continuation of the human Soul and the existence of an afterlife is proven countless times through various forms of Mediumship.

Mind

The vehicle for consciousness.

Nervous system

The system of cells, tissues, and organs that regulates the body's responses to internal and external stimuli. Sensitive nerves through which sensory stimuli pass. Our heightened nervous system perceives on levels of awareness unregistered by the rational mind.

Physical body

The corporeal material self . . . A temporal vehicle for the Soul.

Psychic

An ability of the Soul to sense what is not seen with the physical eyes. A finely tuned awareness of another's energy.

Psychic Reading (A)

Information gleaned by attunement to the person seeking a reading. Our hopes, fears, thoughts and actions, remain within the human aura and are *'Read'* by the Psychic. Strong wishes and desires are interpreted as future events. Clients are impressed with the Psychic's ability to accurately 'Read' them. Information is accessed *without* Spirit presence or assistance.

Psychics and Mediums

All Mediums are psychic, but not all Psychics are Mediums.

Psychometry

The history of an inanimate object, which can be 'read' by a sensitive.

Self, The

The individuality. That, which overcomes the present personality with self-mastery . . . An inner unity that allows the Spiritual Self to direct the life. Consciousness functioning beyond the physical nature and it desires.

Soul

A vehicle for the Spiritual Self

Soul growth

Attributes and creativegifts learned via experience. Spiritual enlightenment that cultures and enriches the indwelling Soul.

Spirit communication

A message relayed via a *mind to mind* attunement between the earthly Medium and a Soul no longer in the confines of a physical body.

Spirit World

The reality where the Soul, Spiritual Self and consciousness exists without the confines of a physical body (see Afterlife)

Spirit communicator. (A)

A consciousness no longer on this earthplane.

Spirit Workers, Coworkers, Colleagues and Friends

Ordinary folk in Spirit who, through their interest in Mediumship and the reality of Spirit communication choose to work, often unappreciated or acknowledged, with a development group.

Spirit Teachers

Souls of varying degrees of spiritual evolvement, who elect to teach and train anyone who seeks spiritual unfoldment.

Spirit Guide, (A)

A longtime companion who remained in the Spirit realms. They walk in harmony with earthly colleagues to fulfill a prearranged plan.

Spiritual Healing

Alleviation of pain and suffering using a Healing Power created by God.

Spiritual Healer

One who is a vehicle for Spiritual Healing. The ability to act as a pure conduit through, which Healing Guides can channel the Healing Power.

Spiritual Unfoldment

What is achieved when the inner journey begins. That which manifests when personal self-discipline and self-mastery take effect.

Spiritual Self

The spark of Divinity in all living things . . . The Kingdom of Heaven within . . . The light of the Soul . . . The Higher Self.

Spirituality

A concern for, and knowledge of, matters of the Spirit. An acknowledgement of God, the Great Spirit, in all things.

The self

The smaller self, the personality before the Spiritual Self is stirred into manifestation.

"Spirituality is . . . an acknowledgement of God, the Great Spirit, in all things."

Janet Cyford

Chapter One

The Family Circle

My mother pined for my father until she became quite ill, but their parting proved to be only temporary. As a fireman in the London Fire Brigade it was impossible for him to join her and the family. It was 1940, the first year of the Second World War and my grandmother, along with several family members, left London to avoid the constant bombing raids. They chose to evacuate to Ilfracombe, a small seaside town on the west coast of England. Unfortunately, it was a disastrous decision, for soon after they settled in, Hitler's airforce began bombing Bristol, an major seaport some miles north of Ilfracombe.

Barely twenty-three years old, my mother was strongly affected by the terror and horror of that time. In later years she often spoke with sadness of the Polish people who, having escaped from Europe, now billeted on the west coast of England. Lists of refugees staying in surrounding areas were displayed in local post offices. New arrivals checked the lists frequently, hoping for news of missing relatives and friends who had been forcibly removed from their homes. With her sisters, she watched and wept as many Europeans reunited, quite by chance, with family members they thought never to see again. Her health, coupled with the difficulties of boarding in a stranger's home decided them, some months later, to take their chances back in London. However, something momentous began during their stay in Ilfracombe. Late one winter afternoon, my mother's elder sister, suddenly, without warning, fell into a deep trance. In later years my aunt told me her story. She and her mother had spent the afternoon talking about spiritual subjects in the same way they had many times before. The crowded, rented room they all shared, was in darkness. Blackout curfew had begun and no sign of interior light must be seen through the heavy black drapes covering each window and doorway. Her last conscious memory was of feeling faint. As the sensation grew, she slipped away to the sound of her own voice begging my grandmother to take care of her. She remembered no more until consciousness returned much later.

Still seated at the dining table she opened her eyes to the sound of my grandmother weeping. During, what my aunt thought was a fainting spell, someone had spoken through her lips, bringing a Spirit message of comfort and support to my grandmother. The messenger encouraged their decision to return to London, reassuring my grandmother of their continuing safety in the bombing raids. My aunt never told me who spoke through her, or if they were recognised, but the experience had a profound effect, on my grandmother and her young daughters. Unharmed by this strange event it nevertheless changed all our lives. This sudden onset of Deep Trance Mediumship manifesting through my aunt that day would continue to improve for the rest of her life. Through the formation of a home circle other family members developed their latent gifts. Furthermore it would continued onwards into other generations.

Chapter Two

Mediumship and the Medium

Mediumship, is the ability to sense and attune to finer Spirit vibrations, unseen by the less sensitive. It is an attribute of the Soul, but its development is not for everyone. Training for every type of Mediumship, takes place on many levels. The physical body must be strong enough to support the heightened nervous system, and the present personality, emotional and mental selves, must be disciplined by the individual's self-mastery.

Not all Mediums develop Deep Trance or Physical Mediumship. Through conscious cooperation with the Spirit teachers who train them, budding sensitives most often develop message Mediumship. Primarily, this is a mental ability used by Spirit to relay evidence of survival beyond the death of the physical body.

Spirit teachers believe, awareness of Spirit is a gift the newborn child carries, a natural ability often evident from early childhood. How this continues to manifest, remains a choice of the indwelling Soul. Its success depends upon the Soul's ability to reflect the Spiritual Self, and its strength to overcome the dictates of the present personality and its current conditions.

Soul culture comes from experiencing, through the personality, the depths of compassion and mercy, understanding and insight, tolerance and patience. These qualities can only be claimed through personal experience. The Soul, as the vehicle for the Spiritual Self attracts circumstances to the physical personality that enable the Soul to grow in spiritual understanding. It can draw from the rich tapestry of experiences, incarnation in the material plane provides. Eventually achieving its goal of unity with the Great Spirit.

Today, there is a greater understanding of individual sensitivity, but there remains many misconceptions, about the ability to communicate with the Spirit world. A Medium does not receive information, from the person who consults them for a private sitting, by mind reading or trick questions. They *do not* attune to the client's mind or their energy. Information is reached for, and received from, a Spirit communicator, a Guide or loved one, wishing to give evidence of their Soul's survival after death.

Public demonstrations of Mediumship have shown, that verifiable evidence of Spirit contact, can be given while the Medium *is unable to see* the audience. In this instance the Medium relies upon an earthly colleague, to locate the recipient of a Spirit communication.

A well-trained Medium consciously cooperates with Spirit and the quality of their gift, depends upon their ability to achieve, perfect and maintain alignment. This elevated degree of attunement is essential to all phases of Mediumship and the mechanics of communication.

Good Mediumship needs one's dedication to the process of development and requires the Medium to be actively involved in the continuing unfoldment of their gift. Therefore, a great deal is expected of the potential Medium before their particular gift is presentable. Even with a natural ability to perceive beyond the normal senses there remains much work to be done, before a Medium can become a strong instrument for genuine communication between both realities. It is vital, for even the most gifted Medium, to learn to govern their sensitivity, before it governs them.

The vibrations a Medium attunes to are on a frequency, which is unavailable to the materialistically focused mind. If one can attune to these frequencies and work in close cooperation with Spirit Guides, a clearer conduit opens between the two vibrations.

We are using a subtly refined perception when the senses extend. To perceive with inner eyes, is not an *extra* sensory perception, but an *extension* of all the senses. Heightened sensitivity to unseen realms, needs constant cultivation and tutoring. If governed with self-mastery it is a rare gift indeed, for to perceive with inner eyes expresses the intuitive power inherent in us all.

There are no short cuts to the development of good Mediumship. Each sensitive is individual, but all share common threads of life experiences. Spirit's cooperation is evident, in the Medium's clairvoyance or clairaudience, Spiritual Healing or Deep Trance Mediumship. Excellence shows in the Medium, who achieves Soul growth and Spiritual Unfoldment along with their mediumistic development.

Spiritual Laws governing communication between the two realities come into effect, when the Medium reaches for a Spirit communicator. The same law, will extract a price if we use our ability unwisely. Our struggle to overcome the smaller self, is even greater for the sensitive whose Mediumship has reached a degree of excellence.

There are moments of pure joy, when many Spirit communicators, blend their thoughts *mind to mind* with the Medium. Evidence of their survival is clearly shown and accepted, by the one seeking news of them. The Medium floats on success for many hours, and the love built during contact, remains tangible, where the private sitting took place.

In these heady moments, never forget, we are only physical telephones receiving and delivering the message. We can *only* accomplish this, with the cooperation of Spirit workers. With humility, we can keep matters in proportion by remembering to thank Spirit coworkers, who make private sittings successful and communication possible.

It is a misconception, to believe the development of Mediumship, bestows instant spirituality along with humility and honesty. All Mediums are very ordinary people, using wisely or unwisely, a rare ability to perceive in another dimension. They too, are struggling to overcome the smaller self and gain self-mastery. We must, therefore, use our personal discernment, to sift information we receive and *appreciate* what is involved in its delivery.

Mostly, our development begins with a sensitivity to another's moods, thoughts and feelings. Two people, who are emotionally attached, find they can anticipate each other's unspoken thoughts. This *rapport,* travels along threads we forge with another.

The same mechanics are used in Mediumship. As our sensitivity blends with the vibration of a Spirit communicator *rapport* begins. Thought travels with ease, along the threads of our attunement. The one in Spirit who wishes to make contact creates in thought, mental imagery, which can be discerned by the Medium. No two sensitives, receive information in quite the same way, but the mechanics involved in Mental Mediumship are the same.

Mediums, speak of seeing and hearing a Spirit communicator, but it is not as simple as this sounds. Images, created by thought, within the Spirit communicators mind, quickly lay upon the reflective surface of the Medium's attuned mind. Speech is heard with something other than the external ear. An auditory sensing comes into play that can detect a speech impediment or foreign accent. Although the impediment or accent is indistinguishable. Using the combination of extended senses, information from a Spirit contact, is *'felt'* with the finer threads of awareness.

There are some Mediums who do not see or hear a Spirit contact, but register a presence and describe in accurate detail, who it is and what they wish to say. Their information comes, with a rapidity that begins with a finer attunement than most sensitives can achieve. It is an accumulation of all the extended senses, working simultaneously in a *clairsentience* that perceives with deeper insight.

If a Medium, remains constantly attuned to finer vibrations, health and mental self suffer. Lacking the self-discipline, to shield and apportion their energy, overuse eventually influences the quality of their gift. A sensitive's energy, needs careful protection. Its ability to absorb information from other sources, can place a strain on the nervous system, leaving them depleted and listless. In sympathy, the sensitive too readily absorbs other people's burdens and unfortunately, are constantly at the mercy of discordant environments.

Chapter Three

Carrying On

Once settled back in London, my grandmother and two of her daughters, formed a regular, weekly home circle for the development of my aunt's Mediumship and to begin their work for Spirit.

One of my earliest childhood memories, is of my father's reaction to the family circle group. He refused to join them in the early days, preferring to baby sit me. Early one evening after the circle began, I left my bed to investigate an unusual sound coming from downstairs. From the staircase, I could see my father lying in the hallway below. His curiosity overcame him and he lay listening at the door of the seance room. Turning to see me standing above him and motioning me to be quiet, he beckoned me down to join him.

We lay in the hallway together eavesdropping on what was taking place within the room. Sadie my aunt's Spirit Guide was always delightful to listen to. Her struggles with the English language and comical expressions were forever part of her charm. On this occasion, much to my father's alarm, she suddenly called his name, saying she knew he was outside the door. I was still very young, but savvy enough to understand, what happened in the circle scared my young father. Heaven knows how he overcame his fear, but from that moment onwards both of us sat in the group with the rest of the family.

He proved to be a natural sensitive and rapidly developed Deep Trance Mediumship. Never regretting joining the circle, he enjoyed his work with Spirit and each circle group was an event to be anticipated. Occasionally, as his gift grew, a Spirit form composed of Ectoplasm would transfigured my father's features and figure. As Spirit operators brought him to his feet, a North American Indian, built rapidly in the condensed energy surrounding him. Standing six feet tall, my father was a very handsome, gentle man. In this physical phenomena the warrior stood even taller. Every detail of the Indian's clothing showed clearly through a deep rose coloured hue. Feathers in his full headdress shimmered as he acknowledged each sitter with a slight nod of his head. Then he slowly disappeared.

As the energy subsided, we sang rousing hymns, knowing Spirit used the energy of our voices to raise the vibrations again. Over many years other Spirit Guides made their presence known and spiritual teaching was given that stimulated our minds to think and reason for ourselves.

The close contact my father developed with his Chinese Guide, was evident as his features changed whenever the Oriental drew near. When my sister was born some years later, my father's nightly task was to stay in our bedroom until the baby fell asleep. He always catnapped while his Oriental Guide spent time talking to me. It seemed very natural, for he comforted and reassured me for the days ahead. Telling me never to fear anything or anyone, he taught me to draw upon the strength of the Spiritual Self within. I did not understand all he taught me then, but his words have returned to remind me many times during my life.

My father worked close to home and the family ate lunch together. Before he returned to his job, he rested in a comfortable chair for forty winks, his midday nap. Sitting on the floor before him, I waited for his Guide to speak to me. His narrow face soon over-shadowed my father's and I could see, a long mustache drooping from either side of his mouth. Memory fails me whether anyone else in the family saw this. I wonder now, if my clairvoyant sight registered changes only seen by me.

We were a very close family, living with my maternal grandmother, who was lovingly known as Nan. Three of my mother's sisters lived close by. Two at the top of our road and one in the next, who was easily reached by a short alleyway. Love extended to our family pets and all joined in every family event. We lived in the heart of London, where World War Two, shaped my formative years. Daily air raids kept everyone in constant fear, wondering whose home would be razed, by the next blitz on London. Fear and anxiety drew families and communities together, to support and watch out for one another.

My presence in the home *circle* during the war, must have been for my safety. Although this was never given as the reason. My mother told me in later years how she had feared for our future. Germany's intended invasion of the British Isles, was a constant threat to the British people and she, along with many other mothers, wondered if her children would be given the chance to grow to full adulthood.

8

Chapter Four

Deep Trance Mediumship and its Development

Groups of people, in different parts of the world were soon rewarded when they gathered in prayer, hoping to speak with loved ones who had made their transition into the world of Spirit. Meeting at appointed times each week, suitable conditions created of love and harmony, enabled the phenomena of Spirit communication to take place.

With dedication and commitment, group members sat in circle, supporting one individual who showed potential for Mediumship. This was most often, Spirit contact through an entranced Medium.

In trance control, a Spirit Guide draws closely to the auric energy surrounding the deeply entranced Medium. With perfect alignment to the nervous system via the spinal column, a closer mind to mind blending occurs. Using the physical apparatus of the unconscious personality, rather than the attuned mind of the conscious clairvoyant, Spirit operators are responsible for maintaining the Mediums heart and pulse rate. In this well conducted process, their priority is the Medium's wellbeing and safety. In this manner, a Spirit Guide could speak directly to all present. They spoke of the Spirit life, the Soul's purpose for incarnation and of universal, Spiritual Laws governing communication between the two worlds.

At the turn of the century conflict and devastation lay ahead, in the form of two world wars. Deep Trance Mediumship provided an avenue for highly evolved Souls in Spirit, to teach from their wisdom and knowledge. A great effort was made to bring humanity to an awareness, of the collision course they were on. Spirit tried to help humankind to change their ways by teaching them to act from their Soul and its inner prompting.

Learning of the Soul's ultimate journey back to the God source, enlightened those who understood the Great Spirit's message. A message relayed by his ambassadors who elected to draw nearer to the earth plane's denser vibrations, endeavouring to raise the conscious-ness of humankind. A willing cooperation from their earthly partner, the trance Medium, permitted these Great Souls to deliver their message first hand.

The same urgent message holds true today. Humanity must raise its consciousness to the Great Spirit for guidance and respond to the outpouring of Spirit energy bathing our earthplane and its inhabitants.

Deep trance Mediumship must not be confused with modern day 'channelling.' The word, channel has become grossly distorted and bears no relationship to Spirit's request that we strive to become clear and pure conduits, in order to be vehicles for the God created power of healing energy. What is promoted as channelling at present, seems to come from the ego's of discarnate or incarnate personalities, overcome with a sense of self-importance. Another alarming aspect of channelling is the practitioners undisciplined willingness to 'channel' all and any consciousness they contact. With no awareness of the danger of being 'used and abused' their altered states of awareness can be likened to one spinning the dial on a radio, or surfing television channels. Once they open themselves to all and any influences the danger increases. Often what is presented as, coming from beyond the light, is nothing more that the ego's joy of self importance.

While Spirit identification is essential when relaying evidence of survival beyond the death of the physical self, it is unnecessary when a Spirit Guide teaches through the medium of deep trance. They may, if asked by members of the circle group, give a name by which we may greet them, but the measurement of their worth is the quality of spiritual teachings delivered in this manner. By their fruits, ye shall know them. However, it is of the utmost importance to the developing Deep Trance Medium to recognize whom and what they are working with. The most important tenet of Mediumship development is to recognize where our information comes from. In this manner we are willing, self-disciplined participants.

* * * * *

Trance Mediums are susceptible to diabetes and other endocrine malfunctions. Self-discipline and the need to quickly replenish protein after a trance session, is rarely understood. When working in altered states of awareness, protein is used rapidly and the physical body needs replenishment. A Medium is not immune to disease because they are doing the work of Spirit. However, the enlivening energy radiating from the Great Spirit, holds the years at bay for many Mediums. This ability to keep the *youth within alive* clearly shows in their stamina to recover from illness and disease.

The development of trance Mediumship needs suitable group members. Sympathetic, understanding people who are willing to lovingly support the trance Medium's faltering steps, as the trance state deepens and grows in strength. Therefore, the circle group is the safest environment for trance development. It is an aspect of Mediumship, open to self-delusion, but with self-knowledge the Medium can prevent negative traits of irritability or rigid opinions, from tainting the Guide's message.

There are several degrees of trance control and the experienced trance Medium may deliver, an inspirational lecture, in a light stage of trance. Voice and mannerisms may remain the same but phraseology differs. Subject matter is delivered with the authority of one who has deeper spiritual knowledge. Although many trance Mediums, prefer the deepest trance that can be achieved, this may in time progress to a perfected, mind to mind, light trance requiring less from the physical energy.

Entrancement is not an enforcement of a Spirit personality, imposing their will upon an unwilling person. Nor is it a state of mind, passively surrendering to unknown influences. Neither is it bodily possession, as some teach in ignorance. The trance state only comes into being through perfect trust and willing cooperation between a Medium and his or her Spirit Guides. It is a cooperation between a Spirit mind and the mind of the trance Medium, which requires a gentle loving awareness and knowledge of their attachment. Deep attunement by both Souls may come from a previous union in other Soul experiences. They are most often, old friends drawn to work together again.

The development circle has many unseen helpers, following directions from the circle's Spirit Guide. His priority is the welfare of the entranced Medium and each group member. It is a smoothly run production, unequaled by any events in our physical world. No doubt, our ego's need for personal recognition, is overcome in the Spirit world. When the trance state has progressed sufficiently and the Guide

11

can speak clearly, instructions may be given, for the development of other Mediumistic gifts.

Trance Mediums must have a disciplined and dedicated approach to their work. Development is an ongoing process and one's gift can always improve. Unfortunately today, commitment and dedication to the process are rare. In our present society we seek instant gratification, lacking patience to cooperate in any lengthy development of intangibles.

A lack of patience brought a decline in the advancement of good vehicles for trance Mediumship. In the past, many fine exponents of this type of Spirit contact, existed in the Spiritualist religion in Great Britain. If a home circle boasted a trance Medium, group members would learn from spiritual teachings, given by the Medium's Guides. In some development circles, no one was allowed to develop spiritual gifts, other than the trance Medium. However, this was not so in my parents' home circle. Two individuals developed deep trance Mediumship, inspirational speaking and clairvoyant sight. There were also, full transfigurations over another circle member. The same circle, produced many fine Spiritual healers who later joined the National Federation of Spiritual Healers, a British organization conducted at that time, by Harry Edwards the Spiritual Healer.

Chapter Five

Early Beginnings

Earlier in this century, many courageous Mediums stood apart and spoke of what they knew to be true in public meetings, Spiritualist churches and at 'Speakers Corner' in a London's Hyde Park. Threatened with prosecution under the Witchcraft Act, they nevertheless trusted a higher power to protect them. Accusations, of doing the work of the devil, continue to be levied by the superstitious and the author wonders how many sensitives today have the courage to stand alone against ridicule and derision.

The dedication of earlier Mediums brought wonderful results. Cooperation with Spirit teachers, enabled them to be ambassadors for the teachings of Spirit. "There is no death," was the message each Medium demonstrated through numerous communications to the loved ones of those who had passed on into the Spirit World.

Using the Medium's trained ability to register their presence, the discarnate communicator proved who they were, with physical descriptions and intimate details of their life on earth. Anxious to let their families know they were well they sought to give proof of their continuing existence in another reality. They told of reuniting with family members who had passed on before them. Obviously, the binding ties of love and friendship, are not severed by the physical separation death brings. Each wanted to tell those left behind, they remained close by and watched over them as before. These earlier requirements of Spirit identification, are no longer appreciated or sought by modern practitioners.

Spirit operators have tried many methods of contact. In 1848, the knocks and raps experienced by the Fox sisters in Hydesville, New York, brought forth investigators of all kinds. Most set out to discredit the phenomena with accusations of fraud. From this time, a widespread interest in Spirit contact, swept across the United States of America and Great Britain. This created opportunities for the development of other mediumistic phenomena. At the turn of the century physical Mediumship was the avenue Spirit chose to prove the existence of an afterlife.

Ectoplasm, the vital energy needed to cloak materialized Spirit forms, could be drawn by Spirit from a certain type of Medium. Spirit workers lovingly protected the Medium from harm. However, they were unable to shield them, from the antagonistic streams of thought, directed by those who wanted to discredit this phenomena with accusations of fraud and dishonesty. Spiritualism was eventually formed as a religion, to protect its Mediums and Healers from persecution and imprisonment.

Genuine and fraudulent Mediums, were thoroughly investigated by researchers not too sure of what they were dealing with. To prevent a Medium hoodwinking the incredulous, investigators secured them in chairs with ropes and sealing wax. Disregarding the humiliation experienced by the Medium, researchers devised more stringent tests to disprove the possibility of Spirit communication and the existence of an afterlife. If the physical Medium's gift was genuine, the most carefully controlled conditions, failed to prevent the appearance of Spirit visitors. Life-size Spirit forms, continued to materialize in the ectoplasm emanating from the deeply entranced Medium. In the safety of the seance room, irrefutable proof of the continuation of life beyond death, was repeated countless times.

The curious and the sensation seeker, demanded a great deal of the Medium's time and energy. This form of Mediumship took its toll on the individual who neglected to take personal responsibility for their wellbeing. If they were not strong minded and failed to discipline their time and energy, their health deteriorated.

During the decades that followed, this frequently misused form of Mediumship became rare, while other types of communication between the two worlds flourished. Modern Mediumship and today's practising Mediums owe a great deal to those earlier Mediums, who endured the indignities of disbelief and ridicule, which often resulted in poor health and early death.

The development of inner clairvoyant sight, was unnecessary to the physical Medium who worked in a deep trance. Circle members, sitting regularly to support the deep trance medium, were firmly discouraged from developing their own clairvoyant sight. Spirit contact today is mostly achieved through mental Mediumship.

Practising Mediums raise their awareness to a heightened vibration, which enables attunement to the consciousness of discarnate Spirit minds.

The gift of true Mediumship is rare, and the ability to give evidence of the human Soul's survival beyond the transition we call death, is rapidly becoming a thing of the past. There is a lack of training in today's practising psychics, for they avoid giving evidence of individual survival beyond death or Spirit identification. Preferring to cloak their psychic ability in variations of *channelling*, they seek personal contact with a higher consciousness that mostly speaks in riddles and is full of drivel. Furthermore, this is presented as the ultimate in spiritual teaching.

Mediums who have retained, developed and governed their sensitivity and inner spiritual sight, oppose certain New Age teachings that declare there is no such thing as individual Spirits. This belief is based on the premise that, each person newly arrived in Spirit, is quickly absorbed into group souls where personality is extinguished. Within these conclusions lies a element of truth, insofar as the Soul's *ultimate* goal, is to be reunited with God, the Great Spirit.

This line of thinking partly echoes the teachings of an established organization and its earlier insistence that, Mediums communicate with nothing more than astral plane, spook shells vacated by those rejoining group souls. Much like the outworn skin shed by a reptile. Maybe this is so, for those who believe it to be so. We certainly create our own reality here and in the afterlife. However, Mediums who find this is not the norm, should stand by what they have found to be true and have the courage to speak openly.

When this conclusion is challenged by the Spirit-trained Medium's ability to distinguish a Spirit communicator from a thought form or projected living image, those that favour absorption, have no acceptable explanation. Our point of view comes from the experiences of modern Mediums agreeing that a Spirit communicator can be easily recognised by the quality of light surrounding them. This degree of light is missing from the projected image of one still alive or a powered up thought form. All reasoning minds would agree that the departed no longer have a physical body with which to show themselves. What appears to the stilled surface of the Medium's mind is the strongly projected thought of how they looked physically while upon the earth. How else can they be recognized?

However, we are told by New Age channelers that what we as Mediums, mistakenly think we are communicating with, is nothing more than astral travellers, who always leave their auric light at home! In this atmosphere of ignorance, is it any wonder sensitives lack the courage to stand for what they know to be true.

Spiritual truths are recognised by their simplicity. Unfortunately, this simplicity is not complicated enough for the intellectual to accept. It is spiritual snobbery at its worst, when ancient truths are reinvented to justify a lack of courage or exorbitant charges for, so called wisdom.

What is so disturbing is the conglomeration of varied systems of thought that are randomly selected and intermingled in present day psychic and spiritual teachings. No one system is thoroughly explored and assimilated. Only that, which suits the individual is accepted and preached as something of value. If the source of what is channelled is unknown and unrecognised by the channeller, who takes responsibility for that, which is given as ultimate truth? We should be careful of what we embrace or reject, always weighing what we hear or read against our own personal discernment.

A study of other belief systems is essential to all Psychic practitioners, working Mediums and modern day Channelers. Religious divisions are crumbling as reasonable people gain insight into other lines of thought, finding common threads of spirituality running through each. It is time to accept that all roads lead to God, and that we can choose which one is suitable to our unfoldment. Expressing our free will in this way we must, nevertheless, be personally responsible for what we teach of our truths, for there are still those who will not think or reason for themselves.

Spirit Guides encouraged us to reason for ourselves. They do not force feed us with only that, which they believe to be true. As teachers they lead their students to the door of the student's inner knowing. If the life of the Soul is continuous, it is reasonable to assume each student can, through inner attunement, access the knowledge their own Soul has gained.

If Mediums learned how their gifts work and the mechanics used by Spirit operators, they could educate others in the simple but natural laws of Spirit communication. Armed with this knowledge, those that grieve and new seekers longing for Spiritual Unfoldment, would be led in safety to their own understanding. It is our personal responsibility, as working Mediums to pass on what we know to be true. That there is no death, and therefore, we will all be reunited once again in the world of Spirit.

Education in this subject, is long overdue. Many misconceptions continue to deride Mediumship and the natural ability of the Medium, as a sensitive, to perceive on other levels of consciousness. The present interest in psychism, has replaced the development of good Mediumship, as many sensitive's remain content to tell fortunes. The Medium differs from the psychic, by their choice to work in cooperation with Spirit. Every sensitive uses an extension of their normal senses. A Medium, however, raises hers to a finer frequency seeking a Spirit communicator, Spirit teaching and Spirit guidance.

Mediumship is the ability to relay evidence, from a loved one in Spirit, to a family member still on earth. The Medium's development comes under the direction of personal Guides, who teach the spiritual laws that govern Spirit communication. Each Medium has life experiences that build self-reliance on an inner strength. They are carefully taught by Spirit to recognize the source of their information. This helps the sensitive to discern genuine Spirit communication, from the idle thoughts of the everyday mind.

Our materialistic approach to life leaves us unaware of any association with the world of Spirit. The physical body obstructs inner spiritual sight and if the consciousness remains dormant in the earthly self, our lives are colourless. Often it is the grief and shock of losing a loved one, that turns us inwardly to seek answers.

After a long journey, our first thoughts upon arrival, are to let the folks back home, know we have arrived safely and all is well. This consideration for loved ones back home, is uppermost in our minds after our transition from this reality into the afterlife. Finding the best method of communicating this simple message, can be difficult. The Medium's task is to deliver the message. Their ability to switch the focus of their consciousness, enables the Medium to reach beyond the normal senses and perceive the presence of a Spirit communicator. The method by which the sensitive receives a message, can vary from Medium to Medium, but its correct delivery free from embellishment, is most important. Communication, brings to the Soul who has made its transition, immeasurable comfort and the grief process eases for those left behind.

Spirit Guides, have shown me there is a Spiritual Self within each of us and it is stirred, when we seek deeper spiritual understanding. It is the key to inner peace and a source of strength, we continuously seek outside ourselves. It will not be found by reading of another's experience and adopting that as our own. It can only be experienced by going within.

The world of Spirit has always been close by. Native people of all lands have known and understood this intuitively. Their knowledge has been systematically destroyed and supplanted with organised religious thought that is devoid of spirituality. Gradually, we are destroying our planet through greed, and materialism has finally blinded us to our source of inner strength. We have little respect for each other, for cultures and lifestyles different from our own, or for any life form on this earth plane. The turmoil in our own nature, now reflects in mother nature.

When human beings deal responsibly with their inner turmoil, mother nature will heal herself. For one is a reflection of the other. We must begin by responding to the spiritual consciousness that is constantly bathing the earthplane. Until we can raise our consciousness, to an awareness of humankind's plight, we will continue to remain in ignorance of our individual contribution to the earthplane's decline.

Chapter Six

Dying to Experience

Knowing, not just believing, there is an afterlife beyond this material existence, helped me to deal with the deaths of those who mattered most to me. Therefore, I have the utmost compassion, for people who do not embrace this knowledge. How do they cope with the reality of death, believing they will never see a loved one again? The magical transformation of sorrow, evidence of survival brings, relieves the one who grieves and releases or unburdens, the one who has passed into the world of Spirit.

When contact is made through a Medium, it is with the purpose of assuring those left behind that he who died, still exists. No longer in a physical shell, for the life force withdrew from the body at death, but in a body of light that allows the consciousness to still function, albeit in another vibration. Strengths of character and quirks of personality are as before death. No one sprouts wings and becomes instantly angelic. What died was the physical body, the overcoat of the individual we knew, what survived was their Spiritual Self, Soul and all its experiences. Newly arisen in consciousness and freed from the confines of the material world, we nevertheless remain the same beyond death and must face ourselves accordingly.

The manner in which we die, is a fear everyone faces. Wondering how painful death will be adds to our dread of growing old. Fear of death fills our consciousness with images of suffering as does a predilection for science fiction and horror stories. When fear becomes greater than reason, our Greater Self must struggle to take control at the time of death. Having the courage to move through life with certainty towards the final transformation, comes only with an inner knowing of our true spiritual nature. As intelligent reasoning people, we have a responsibility to remove from our minds, all thoughts that contribute to our fear of the unknown. Only trust in a higher power can quieten these fears, for there is nothing to fear, but fear itself.

Believing the consciousness remains to experience burial or cremation after death burdens many lives. This illogical, but very human fear brings moments of panic when thoughts of death haunt the terminally ill. These and other horrors also torment the newly bereaved as they deal with the sudden or prolonged passing of a dearly beloved child, partner or parent. Only the testimony of those returning to share their experience can ease the burden of grief and allay our fear of the unknown.

Our thoughts are living things. With the power of thought, we create our own reality here and in the afterlife. The ease of our passing from this physical reality, will be pleasant or distressing depending upon what we believe to be true. Someone who is firmly entrenched in the notion that death is as prolonged and difficult as birth, will experience this to be so. Those who are free of religious dogma, who think, reason and rely upon their inner knowing, face and experience death with peace and tranquillity.

During sleep, our consciousness switches its focus from the physical reality to function for a short period in another vibration. It is the partially released consciousness that meets a loved one during our sleep state. Death of the physical body fully releases our consciousness to function from then on, in the world of Spirit. It also removes all conscious sensation and feeling awareness of the physical body. All that remains of the rapidly ebbing life force shows in the diminishing auric field. The golden bowl of the physical vehicle shatters and the silver cord slowly separates.

What can we expect after our release from the physical shell? No one returns to say they found themselves in darkness, or alone and afraid. Nor do they speak of passing through a tunnel towards a great light, something that seems to be peculiar to near-death experiences. Mostly, they return during a private sitting, accompanied by the person in Spirit who met them as death took place. As the consciousness expanded and released them from their earthly body, relatives in Spirit embraced them in reunion. No one is alone at the moment of death, many Spirit workers' gather to assist even though we believe a loved one's death was sudden and unexpected.

Attempting to give evidence of themselves, some communicators relate the circumstances leading to their death. Depending on certain degrees of sensitivity, the deceased person's physical health at the time of death, can be sensed by the Medium. A missing limb, a confused senile mind, or the ravages of Cancer or Aids, register upon the sensitivity with amazing clarity, although the Medium has no personal life experience of these things. The affects of ill health remain clearly etched in their Soul memory and some have difficulty relating their experiences dispassionately for the strong memories are painful to relive.

A Medium of some reputation and long years of experience asked me to give her a private reading. My first communicator was the medium's mother. When I said, " I have a lady here who tells me she is your mother" the medium corrected me very forcibly. She told me not to be so silly, her mother had died many years before and would have long gone on. I didn't bother to ask her to what her mother had gone on to. It is not of my experience that our loved one's 'go on' in their progression to some state that is beyond our reach.

Death does not sever the links of love and friendship between us. These links bind us together for eons of time. In the same vein, many choose to believe that we are holding our loved ones back by wanting to communicate with them after they have passed from this material world. Hold them back from what? The progression that is open to every Soul, on its journey back to God, is one of understanding and Soul development . . . not of location. It has been my experience, that our excessive grief can burden them, but it does not impede their Soul growth. Trying to penetrate the cloud of grief surrounding the bereaved poses a very real problem for the recently departed. As they draw near to impinge thoughts of comfort on their loved ones their very presence invokes more tears. Processing grief is necessary for our mental and emotional wellbeing but we have a long way to go before each of us, in our personal loss, can celebrate the reunion taking place in the Spirit realms between our loved one and those that have passed on before.

We do our loved ones a great disservice, when we repeatedly rerun, all the gory details that led to their death. Thoughts are living things and we constantly draw those we love back into these memories. Consider the ramifications of reliving gunshot wounds that took your life and ruined the lives of those dear to you. Of being drawn back into these sensations every year on the anniversary of your death. John F. Kennedy died in this way and with morbid repetition, the media reruns film footage of the tragic event. A slew of new books appear with regularity, rehashing his life and the method

21

of his assassination. In sympathy, we can imagine how his loved ones feel, but who can say what horror he is made to re-experience annually.

Recalling joyful memories of our loved ones raises them into the light of understanding and illumination. In love, we must not fetter them by constantly recalling painful memories of their faults, sicknesses or suffering.

Chapter Seven

Dangerous Times

My family attended a local Spiritualist Church in a North East suburb of London. In the years following the war, they held elected positions of President, Treasurer, Secretary and served as committee members. They would be associated with this church until my father died forty years later.

The church stands on land, purchased with money donated to the Spiritualist Movement by Sir Arthur Conan Doyle, author and creator of Sherlock Holmes. He was a great advocate of Spiritualism and a contemporary and friend of Arthur Findlay. The Findlay mansion, willed at his death to be used for Psychic Studies, is now the headquarters of the Spiritualist National Union.

During the war, our Spiritualist Church did not escape incendiary bomb damage. Until repaired, services were held in our home. This simple row house in London, became an open doorway between our physical world and the world of Spirit.

Most of the Mediums who went on to make their mark in Spiritualism, visited this small church. They became friends and acquaintances of my mother and her family. When everyone was much older, I would meet and work with many of them.

Through the deep trance Mediumship of my aunt, Spirit promised our safety. With the utmost trust in their promise the circle members met regularly throughout the war years even if there was an air raid! We survived those dangerous times and were saved from harm in the relentless bombing raids. Spirit intervened again sometime before Nan, my grandmother had a close call with death.

A particularly insidious German invention, crossed the English channel daily. In great numbers they were aimed at strategic points in London. It was a light, pilotless aircraft, filled with explosives destined for the dock lands and business district of the City of London. Without the precision of modern technology their targets could not be guaranteed and huge numbers drifted into London's residential suburbs. The loud noise of the aircraft's engines, could be heard soon after an air raid warning. Londoners', held their breath until the monster passed overhead and out of sight. Danger began, when the engines stopped. With an unearthly scream the aircraft began its rapid descent to the ground. Its path of destruction was enormous. In the final blast, shops, factories, schools, hospital or houses would be levelled, killing or burying the occupants alive.

My mother was prompted to warn Nan repeatedly, of a plan of action she devised. If she were in the marketplace and saw an aircraft descending, Nan was to run towards it. The prophetic advice must have come from Spirit and Nan used it to save her life.

Rationing shortages, made food shopping a nightmare. What little appeared in the few remaining shops, sold rapidly. News of deliveries, to green grocers, butchers and fishmongers, quickly passed by word of mouth through each neighbourhood. On this summer morning, Nan left home to hurry several blocks to try her luck at the fishmongers. Crowds of people waited in line to buy fish, the first delivery for sometime. They queued, while the air raid warning sounded and still remained in line, as the dreaded aircraft noise drew nearer.

When the engines finally stopped, the aircraft could be seen making a rapid descent along the High Road towards the fishmongers. Tail flames ignited stores on either side of the road, until it finally crashed, burying the fishmongers' customers and levelling surrounding buildings. At home my mother crouched over me in our garden air-raid shelter. We felt the explosion soon after the aircraft's engines cut out and mother said she knew it had fallen near by . . . but, where was my grandmother Nan?

She returned home to her franticly distraught family many hours later; dishevelled, her clothes covered in blood, exhausted and tearful from shock. She had used all her strength comforting the injured she pulled from the rubble and was now near to collapse. My grandmother was one of few unharmed, for she remember my mother's plan and ran *towards* the oncoming plane . . . which passed over her head to explode where she had been standing in the long queue to buy fish.

Chapter Eight

Firm Foundations

The Mediumship of my mother, father and aunt grew rapidly and Spirit phenomena happened regularly in our weekly home circle. When my school days began, it surprised me to find, no other child had these wonderful things happening at home. I instinctively knew, to keep silent about my Spirit friends. Overwhelmed, by the noisy rough and tumble of school life, I tried hard from a very young age to govern my sensitivity. In later years, I learned by associating with many other Mediums, their sensitivity had also given them some bad moments in childhood.

My early education in spiritual truths came from Spirit Guides. Sadie, a Spirit friend, spoke to us through the deep trance Mediumship of my aunt. She was a young African girl, with a deep love for all of us. There are many unasked questions, about her connection to my family and how she chose my aunt to work with, but we knew of her devotion to us. When my aunt's health and age prevented her trance work, Sadie remained with her until she died and they reunited in Spirit. Sadie also had a deep love for my mother Irene, whom she affectionately called Tulla. Spirit's plan had been for Tulla to develop deep trance Mediumship, but this was abandoned by her Guides, because of her serious heart disease.

What now seems most remarkable, was then commonplace and a matter of acceptance. Our lives were intimately involved with Spirit and we turned to them for advice, looking upon them as family members. This intimate relationship with many Spirit people who spoke regularly with us, continued into my adult years, when their guidance and support helped me to deal with equally disruptive problems.

A Scottish Terrier puppy was given to me for my fourth birthday and Sadie named her Moy-yo. She explained this African name meant,

25

old faithful. The dog's name got shortened to Mog, but she would always be remembered for her faithfulness. Sadie taught me the Lord's Prayer. Leaning against my mother's lap, I repeated the words she spoke through my deeply entranced aunt. When Sadie became very tongue-tied and unable to explain herself clearly, an amazing thing happened. Her girlish voice changed mid-sentence into that of a man we knew as Bill. The tone and depth of his deep voice could not be mistaken for Sadie's girlish one. Gently teasing her, he unravelled her meaning and allowed her to continue. They worked very closely together, he helping her to clearly express what she had come to say.

During deep trance sessions, while my aunt was oblivious to what passed through her lips, Sadie, with Bill's help gave evidence of life after death to a multitude of people seeking the comfort of a Spirit communication. There were many, newly arrived in the Spirit world, desperate to ease the grief of their family members. The war had taken them so tragically and young airmen, sailors and soldiers, returned with Sadie's help to tell their grieving parents they were okay. My aunt's Mediumship flourished in time to be the voice for so many.

Spirit teachings, were always the topic of conversation, when my mother and aunt got together. My aunt often experienced Spirit's presence as she settled to sleep. During these passive moments, Spirit strengthened their link with her and she received their teachings. Early the next day, she hurried to our house as soon as she could, eager to share her latest experience with her many Spirit companions. My grandmother Nan made tea and we sat at the kitchen table ready to hear my aunt's tale. This always led to further discussions of the wonderful implications of Spirit communication.

These were precious moments for me as the subjects were always spellbinding. Lack of understanding, or my young age, never excluded me from the discussion. They talked of the reality of life after death; and how intimately involved, the Spirit world is with our material one. One of my favourite subjects was conception!

When did the Soul enter the physical shell? Was it at conception, quickening, or at the time of birth? They reached no conclusion but it remained a subject for discussion for many years. Discussions continued in circle, when a Guide gave different points of view teaching us to reason for ourselves. This will confuse those who believe there can only be one answer to important questions. Spiritual

Laws govern all matters, but humankind's personal free will, constantly overrides these laws.

When does the Soul enter the physical shell? Spirit teaches, that the Soul's entry varies according to circumstances. The material body being formed may not be strong enough, to support the incoming Soul's plans, and this could result in a miscarriage. A Soul may hesitate until later in the gestation period, when the mother's health, or circumstances had improved. Sometimes, a Soul will enter the physical shell at the time of birth. Another may change their mind exercising free will but lacking courage for the life ahead.

Spirit companions assured us, the Divine hand is always close by, for it is not the Will of God that brings tragedy, but our expression of our free will. My family blessed my life for their spiritual understanding provided fertile ground for my sensitivity to grow in safety. Spiritualism, a Lyceum Sunday school and the Mediumistic phenomena in our home circle, gave an excellent foundation for my Soul growth and later Mediumistic development.

My parents gave us the freedom to choose our religious loyalties. They did not force-feed either of their daughters with their religion, Spiritualism. My mother often reminded us, we were free to choose another religion if we wanted to, we had her blessing. Her gifts were Spiritual Healing and a knowledge of spiritual subjects, that came from her Soul's far memory. She held the position of Mediumship secretary at the local Spiritualist Church for twenty five years. This involved arranging for visiting Mediums to conduct the twice weekly church services. She had compassion and understanding for others and strongly identified with young people, whom she felt had a raw deal as they struggled through their teenage years.

Her personal qualities, drew many young people to her. In later years, when her health confined her to her home she arranged youth groups. Several young people gathered to listen to Mediums speak of their experiences of Spirit and how they came to believe in an afterlife. On other occasions Guides spoke to us, while their instrument the Medium, remained in deep trance. Others demonstrated clairvoyance by giving personal messages to the gathering. My mother touched many people's lives in this way and through her weekly discussion group. The discussion group continued for a long time and was a source of frustration and satisfaction to her. Her frustration came with those who would not reason for themselves and followed, like sheep, the strangest ideas. Satisfaction came from seeing the comfort spiritual teachings bring, to someone who grieved for a loved one or feared their own death.

Her work continues through her close association with my work today. I look upon her as my master of ceremonies operating from Spirit. She heads the team that works with me in each private reading that takes place and I rely upon her to gently school each communicator in the method and mechanics of mind to mind attunement necessary for this to take place. Her input in my group work, lectures and seminars is beyond price. Strangely, I sometimes find myself grieving for her life and how her health restricted her so. I know she was not aware of her part in forming my character until she passed to that next reality, or how her inner strength was to support me in later years.

Chapter Nine

The Seven Principles of Spiritualism.

Seven principles form the cornerstone of Spiritualism. They were taught to me during my Sunday school days at a Lyceum Spiritualist Church in London. The principles were six in number when given from Spirit, through the deep trance Mediumship of Emma Hardinge Britten an American Medium. The Spiritualist National Union adopted the principles in 1901. On the advice of solicitors, they were reworded for the purpose of legal definition, and became known as the Seven Principles. They are as appropriate today as they were then, for they give a spiritual code to live by.

1. The Fatherhood of God.

Spirit never defines God as a cruel or unforgiving authority, but as a supreme power accessible to everyone. Therefore, the Great Spirit is not personified as an authoritative parent dispensing reward and punishment. But as a collection of goodness, an energy of love and light, a God energy to which we all belong. This same energy of goodness lives in each of us. It is the Spiritual Self that seeks expression through the Soul. It is the light of the Soul. The Self that unfolds when we choose to align with its power and say "Thy will not mine." The goodness we call God manifests by Spiritual Law. We can live by the law, but we cannot change it. The highest Spiritual Law is love. Love that is unconditional, nonjudgmental and embraces and respects all forms of life.

The promised Kingdom of Heaven can be found within, but our quest for Spiritual Unfoldment begins when we have enough courage to journey to the very centre of our being. In the inner room of the heart we may meet with our spark of the Divine. Ever present, it has accompanied the Soul through all its experiences, waiting patiently for the outer personality to remember its spiritual heritage. This Spiritual Self must be stirred, awakened and allowed to manifest in our lives. God's gift to humankind was freewill and until we align our free will with the God force and acknowledge the Spiritual Self, the Divinity within us remains dormant.

Every religion speaks of the spark of God within all living things and points the way to the inner journey. Until we know the *Self* and can access the power within, we shall continue to search for spiritual direction outside ourselves. We are made in God's image because we hold the same Divinity within us. Until we allow the dormant God energy to manifest in our lives, we remain poor representations of the goodness of the Great Spirit.

2. The Brotherhood of Man

We are entering the age of Aquarius, an age of mental activity that is already bringing advances in worldwide communications. Without leaving our homes we can access information along waves of energy transmitted through the ether. Humanitarian principles must be paramount in order to counterbalance rapid technological advances that are soulless. The pictorial image that represents the sign of Aquarius, shows a biblical figure pouring water from a jug. As all symbolic pictures hold deeper meaning a closer look reveals waves of thought streaming from the receptacle held by the figure. This ancient wise one, replenishes humankind with the spiritual nourishment of thought. Not the linear thinking of the personality's materialistic mind, but the higher mind's non-linear acceptance of the unity of all things. Uranus, the planet coupled with this air sign, is the symbolic representation of higher thought, thought waves transmitted through ether. Where Mercury is the messenger of the Gods, Uranus lets us deal directly with God by experiencing our own spark of Divinity. Uranus is the higher octave we must raise our consciousness to.

The Brotherhood of hu-Man-kind, is of the Spirit, not of gender. It recognises each human being, irrespective of race, colour, gender or creed, as being part of one another, united by the spark of Divinity we each hold. The spiritual power of the Aquarian Age, demands that the least of us is raised in consciousness before, we as a human race, can achieve spiritual progression. We must respect and care for one another for this is the Soul's expression of the law of love. Realizing our spiritual connection to the Great Spirit and to each other, we recognize we are a family of Humankind.

The Piscean Age should have taught us how to achieve the Christ consciousness within, by emulating the life and teachings of the man Jesus. History records the atrocities done in the name of Christianity while this Great Soul continues to suffer for our misinterpretation of his wonderful teachings. He lived in harmony with all living things and his healing miracles used the natural laws of Spirit and nature. Knowing that the kingdom he spoke of was within himself, this great prophet showed the way for human-kind to live. Asking that we do unto others as we wished to be done by, his teachings were simple and could be used by all. By emulating his ways we could all experience the Kingdom of Heaven within.

Now, in this coming era, we must learn to live more lightly upon the earth, requiring less and giving more. Humankind's materialistic greed, for acquisition at the expense of others, will not escape the spiritual laws of cause and effect. As we destroy the air we breathe and the earth and seas that support our existence circumstances will force each human being to raise their consciousness to the plight of all living things. By taking personal responsibility now for our own thoughts and actions we can avoid further damage. But this must begin with each individual. We can seek dominion over our smaller 'self' by constantly raising the creative life force above the belt. Here the divine fire can awaken the higher centres of awareness.

As a human race we have a great debt to pay for our lack of respect towards the animal kingdom and mother earth, however, both will survive without us. For these things are also governed by spiritual laws, which eventually balance all wrong doings.

The greatest gift we can give another, is freedom to discover who they really are. Coupled with encouragement to celebrate their uniqueness. When we respect each person we are expressing the brotherhood of the spirit. Promote self-esteem in each child and discourage competitiveness, for this destroys family love and respect. Display kindness, gentleness and see these qualities as character

31

strengths, for they are gifts of the Spirit. Reward honesty and integrity as the highest ideals we can attain and give perfect freedom to all to work towards these goals. Emulate the hero and heroine who brings these qualities to their careers, politics, religion and family life. Celebrate these deeds, for they are the marks of an evolving Soul.

3. The Communion of Spirits and the Ministry of Angels

Personal communion with the world of Spirit is a natural phenomena understood by the indigenous people of all nations. Spirit life is intimately involved with our own. Loved ones who have passed on, remain part of our family. Their death has not severed the ties of love we have with them. When in distress, they try to comfort us in the same way they did when alive.

They do not lose their identity or individuality as some schools of thought teach, but remain no further away than a thought. Of course the life of the Soul continues in growth, always seeking the light of understanding, but their connection to us as loved ones is never severed.

At the very moment of death many gather to meet the Soul as it awakens in its new reality. Assistance also comes from deeper levels of Soul existence and sincere prayers are responded to by beings who have passed beyond the confines of personality and ego. This hierarchy, ministers to all levels of being. Working within Spiritual Law, their hands extend to help, guide and direct. Angelic qualities of patience, understanding and compassion, show these Souls to be God's messengers.

4. The Continuous Existence of the Human Soul

The inner self acknowledges the human Soul's immortality. On an intuitive level we know we have been, we are, and we will always be. As the Divinity within directs our feet to a spiritual path an understanding of our goal unfolds. All experiences, even those we feel are negative, are part of the Soul's journey towards perfection. Finally experienced when the Soul is reunited with the Godhead, its source.

Death's transition does not separate us from those we love. The grave receives only the outworn physical overcoat. The very essence of one's selves, personal characteristics, consciousness, Soul and Spiritual Self, passes into the world of Spirit and continues to be. Never fear, that loved ones will reincarnate and not be there to greet you in Spirit, when God calls you home. There are many experiences for the Soul but none of these will separate us from those we love.

Ties of love transcend all levels of being, stretching across our earthly conception of time and space. In the Spirit world as we think of a loved one, there they are, for thought is a powerful, living thing. Reincarnation is a choice the Soul can make. It is not God's Will that we return to earth immediately or if ever. When on earth we are encased in physical matter. The Soul and Spiritual Self are bound in a body of flesh, not their natural state of freedom. It is said this earthly sojourn is one of the most difficult experiences for the Soul because of its lack of freedom.

5. Personal Responsibility.

Use common sense in your search for spiritual awareness. The reader has a responsibility to assess the written word. If that, which you are reading, insults your intelligence, put it aside and seek other experiences. Personal Guides will lead you to your own understanding.

Do not consult Mediums or Psychics, placing upon them the responsibility for decisions, you should be making. Under Spiritual Law you are accountable for your thoughts and actions. No one can absolve you of that, which you alone are responsible for.

Taking personal responsibility for deeds of commission and omission, brings an alignment with the Soul's purpose and allows the Spiritual Self to manifest in our lives. Monitor your thoughts, for they are living things. They attract, similar and sympathetic thoughts to you. Thought accumulates by association with like-minded thoughts. If ours are full of anger, vengeance and malice we attract similar condition's full of the same characteristics. We create our own reality by our thinking. Consider the power of prayer, it too, is cumulative and can accomplish wonderful things.

Be responsible for what you share with others. Do not fill their ears with your understanding, but lead them to the door of their inner wisdom. Permanent damage can be done by the rigid minds of those who feel they alone hold the final truth. Spirit Guides will always teach in a way that challenges us to think and reason for ourselves. But they will not reinforce opinions that leave no room for our growth.

6. Compensation and Retribution for All Good and Evil Deeds done on Earth.

Sometimes retribution or reward rebounds quickly and the scales of justice are seen to be balanced. In other circumstances the crime goes unpunished, or so it seems. As the man Jesus said, "Do unto others as you would be done by," for all personal actions face us when we pass to Spirit. We must judge and condemn ourselves, once we realize the far reaching effects of our actions. When we can look with honesty at the results of our selfish ways, unkind thoughts and deeds, we need to apologize to 'our loved ones', before any further Soul progression can be made. Reflecting upon life now gives us time to make amends to those whom we have hurt, directly or indirectly. It is difficult to do so once we are in Spirit. Without the physical shell we cannot hide who we really are. Guilt colours our appearance, for each thought and deed reflects in the surrounding light of the Soul. It is then clear for all to see, how our words, indifference and cold aloofness wounded and hurt others.

The full rippling effect of our actions can only be fully understood through the eyes of the Soul. When reviewing the life record, the Soul judges itself. It must make amends to those it harmed, before finding brighter light. If we fulfilled selfish desires at the expense of another's wellbeing, we must restore the balance before another step is taken. Many Spirit communicators come to apologize to those they should have loved with more understanding. They ask to be forgiven for their ignorance and indifference to the far reaching effects of their actions. Is it possible that the one who inflicted pain or laughed at another's challenge, will find himself in similar circumstances, in another Soul experience?

The overbearing personality, intent on fulfilling its own wishes, continually rides-roughshod over others. This sets in motion, patterns that are difficult to alter. Manipulation of another's free will is an infringement of Spiritual Law. Idle gossip brings a similar punishment, equal to the damage done by the gossiper. So many Souls have their characters assassinated in this manner. It is the whispering game, as it is repeated it becomes distorted and embellished out of all proportion.

Our thoughts create our reality and once thought turns to inquiry the Soul responds to any changes we make to improve our ways. Far better to seek greater awareness of our actions here, while still in the physical realm.

There are Spiritual Laws that govern Spiritual Unfoldment. Man, Know Thyself is the first requirement. Until we know ourselves how can we understand another? If you wish to develop spiritual understanding, insight and compassion, beware of your conduct towards others. The mark of a truly evolving Soul shows in the respect and regard they have for other human beings.

7. **Eternal progress open to every Soul.**

Spiritual Law applies on all levels of existence. As above, so below. This particular Spiritual Law fulfils all human rights. In the world of Spirit every Soul has an opportunity to evolve along chosen pathways. All individual Souls are important and there is a lack of gender preference in Spirit's teaching, for neither male nor female is esteemed one above the other. When the higher *Self* craves expression, it eventually supersedes the needs of the smaller self. We can choose to seek the light of understanding while in the material world or when the Soul is ready for further progression in Spirit.

A lack of understanding of its true spiritual nature can block Soul growth during the life spent in the physical world. However, the Soul draws to itself experiences that will discipline the earthly personality into recognizing the wisdom and knowledge that lies within. If we have been motivated by material gain throughout our life, the need for ownership is difficult to overcome once we are in Spirit.

This earthly experience can be likened to attending a vast university where our Soul chooses subjects to excel in. It may take eons of time to reach a degree of perfection and we will be well tried, tested and examined. The curriculum includes subjects unknown to our universities. Qualities of unconditional love and compassion, are gained by insight that brings patience. Gentleness is the reward for selflessness, fortitude and courage. In the eyes of Spirit, the accomplishments of the Soul are only learned through experience.

Gaining an understanding of these qualities, is only the beginning; then the Soul must be tested to strengthen its weaknesses. These moments of testing may be the most significant and transforming periods of our life here on earth. When the Soul expresses more of its spiritual nature, the need to take on an earthly physical personality ceases. It chooses experiences in other vibrations and eventually evolves to a state of being, which is formless. It has then moved a little nearer to its goal to be at-one-ment with God.

35

"Death does not sever the ties of love we have with one another."

Janet Cyford

Chapter Ten

The Rescue Circle

A very interesting development began, when Spirit asked my family to form a Rescue Circle. I never took part by sitting in on any session, so my knowledge of finer details is sketchy. My father taped some sittings, but they recorded poorly and were difficult to listen to. My mother and aunt worked perfectly together for these sessions and I can only admire the trust they had in each other and their Spirit colleagues.

Opinions vary as to what qualifies as a rescue circle. Some believe there must be violent individuals rescued and strong circle members to physically restrain the deep trance Medium, being used by the Soul in need of rescuing. Anything less ranks as, giving a helping hand, not rescue work. No doubt, others have witnessed in their rescue circles, violence that needed restraining. Spirit is always concerned with the safety of the entranced Medium and it is inconceivable, that they would expose their Medium's delicate nervous system, to such stress. In cases of extreme violence, I feel the trance Medium's need for histrionics should be questioned.

Violence was not the norm in this home circle, although, some loud and vulgar language took place! Spirit workers carefully orchestrated each event, and my aunt, the deep trance Medium, came to no harm. The cooperation needed by all concerned came from a deep abiding trust in each other's capability.

Family members told the story of a drug addict, whom Spirit coworkers brought to my aunt. While she was deeply entranced, he spoke through her. The amount of time he had been in Spirit is unknown, but, during that time he had remained in the darkness of his own making. Spirit workers tried explaining his present condition to him, but he laughed at them. Until an addict agrees to leave their *mind created* environment, not much can be done. It is difficult to convince them of their death, for the conditions they continue to experience are founded on their last earthly memory. So, they choose to remain in the gutter or alleyway awaiting the next fix. Many wonderful Souls in Spirit, go into the dark places created by those addicted to their conditions. They try to comfort them before and after the drug induced death.

Maybe, this young man had agreed to come and meet some people, who would help him. Bringing him into the Medium's energy, allowed him to experience the physical world's density again and this may have convinced him.

The gentle voice of my mother, explaining who she was and why he was there, did much more. She asked him questions and said comforting things. However, there were some difficult moments, when he questioned her sanity. He wanted to know why were they sitting in the bathroom! She explained, this large room had recently been converted into a bathroom. As it was the quietest room in the house, they always held the family circle there.

Maybe the absurdity of the surroundings, helped to open his mind. The tiniest glimmer of light, breaks the rigid mind and allows Spirit's help to filter through. I do not know his name or who he was. After my mother died in 1975 she returned to tell us of a young man whom she had befriended in Spirit. He had died of a drug overdose and they are still friends today.

* * * * *

Minnie was a true cockney woman, with a strong liking for anything containing alcohol. This craving remained with her after she died and trapped her in a mindset of her own making. The dynamics of her sudden attachment to my aunt are unusual. My teetotaller aunt, suddenly found herself with a craving for a bottle of sherry, she happened to find long forgotten in the sideboard. Contrary to popular belief, a Spirit trained Medium is not easily overshadowed, by the wishes of determined discarnate minds. Especially when that mind wishes to experience something that is abhorrent, to the one they want to influence. Life experiences have taught them to listen to no other, but God and his ambassadors. And to be aware of the source of such influences. There is a vast difference, between the willing passivity of deep trance and the loss of control and willpower in possession. The former happens with loving cooperation and the latter through the attraction of like-mindedness. Maybe, Spirit found this the easiest way to prompt my aunt to arrange a circle sitting. For this is what she did, after telling my mother of the craving that bothered her for several hours.

After the usual instructions from the Chinese Guide who conducted the circle, Minnie breezed in. Speaking through my aunt Minnie admitted it had been her strong cravings, that led to the discovery of the liquor. She apologized if she had been a nuisance. The bitter unhappiness of her own life led to her to drink excessively and she eventually died in dreadful circumstances, caused by her alcoholism. She knew she was dead but things were no better for her; for she remained trapped in the rigid mindset of her own unhappiness.

Asking her to think of her own mother, brought forth a string of obscenities, as she remembered "that old cow" who treated her like a servant. My mother asked her to try to see the light. "What bleeding light" Minnie wanted to know, for she could not see any such thing. My mother's gentle voice remained unshaken, as she explained it was the light of understanding that would come when she forgave her mother. She did not know how to forgive her, so my mother suggested they asked God to help. Minnie said she never prayed to God for help, because she "didn't need any bloody help."

Assuring her it was very simple to do, my mother offered to pray for her, and Minnie finally agreed. As my mother asked God to help this Soul who was so lost, Minnie exploded, denying she had ever been lost. My mother firmly insisted, she was indeed lost, and the beautiful prayer continued. Never doubt the power of sincere prayer for it achieved the lift Minnie needed to see her mother, who had always been close by, waiting for a chance to reach her daughter.

* * * * *

Suitable conditions in the circle group, can be used, to bring someone in Spirit who is in need of help. This situation does not require the gift of deep trance Mediumship and members of the group, may not be aware of the extra visitor's presence. Bringing a Soul, who is unable to accept they have died, helps them to come to terms with their transition. It is comforting for them to see that death did not severed their connections to this reality. Accompanied by Spirit coworkers, many come to watch the work accomplished in a well-run group. This piques their curiosity to learn more of the nature of Spirit and matter. Occasionally, Spirit coworkers enlist the help of a group member.

By allowing the one in Spirit to draw closer during a group exercise, a student registers details of this person's appearance and the mind to mind images they send. When the student relates what they have received, it confirms for the Spirit contact that, with the help of Spirit colleagues, they can communicate with this plane of existence.

There are instances of soldiers trapped in the circumstances of their deaths, their minds endlessly repeating the details of their experience. Prayer and the tireless efforts of wonderful Souls in Spirit, eventually dispels their darkness. The quality of light needed to lift fear and anger from those who cannot move beyond their experience, comes from ordinary people in Spirit. Choosing to help, their act of kindness and compassion, enables the Soul to evolve nearer to its source, the Godhead.

It is beneficial to the Spirit, who cannot overcome a life ruined by the inhumanity of others, to receive help from a willing companion, still in the physical body. Some years ago, my mother asked if I would help a young man, who still suffered greatly from the cruelty of the Nazi regime. She said we were similar in character and she felt my way of life and knowledge of the afterlife, would help him. As an afterthought, she assured me, it was unnecessary for he and I to have long conversations. By introducing him to me, Spirit hoped for some improvement, in this young man's overwhelming sorrow.

Over a period of several weeks, I was aware of him clairvoyantly and he slowly revealed some details, of his short life on earth. He was the eldest son of a middle-class Jewish family of Belgian origin. His family were displaced and eventually scattered to various inhuman deaths. His father a silversmith, was taken from his young family and never heard of again.

The most poignant moment of his presence, happened while I was preparing a chicken for Sunday lunch. I found myself obsessed with its freshness and washed it thoroughly several times. Suddenly aware of my young Jewish friend's voice, I listened as he described a fetid, maggot-ridden chicken, his mother tried to salvage to feed her starving family. His thoughts were so strong, they impinged on my feelings and the chicken suffered another cleaning.

He was obsessed with food for his young body had been denied nourishment for a long time. I never learned how he died, it seemed too cruel to ask, but in the sharing of minds I think I knew too well what had happened to him. The clairvoyant pictures I received of him were very clear. He always showed himself in the battered, threadbare, black overcoat he had huddled in. This was a situation where a young Soul arrived in Spirit and reunited with his family members. He knew they were all safe now and free from harm. However, his strong will used to show and tell me his story, had him trapped in outrage and anger. Sorrow overwhelmed him, he needed to heal his memories before he could be expected to forgive his persecutors. His visits grew less and less and I wondered if I had helped him in any way. When asked, my mother said he was now coping well and freeing himself of bitterness.

One wonders about the road ahead, for this young man and thousands more, who were subjected to the overpowering despotic will of another. Whether he will seek revenge for his sorrow or use his experience as a Soul initiation is his choice. Having known him for a short while, I believe he will go beyond his very real distress, for this stems, not from his own ill treatment but the suffering of those he loved.

It takes will power to rise above the past. To do so the will must be aligned with the will of the Great Spirit. Equally so, the personal will could choose to seek revenge. Here in the latter choice, lies the answer to the uprising of brute force, that accompanies many generations. Within the Spiritual Law of Attraction, like-minded bullies gather in group consciousness, to perpetuate what was unfulfilled during the last incarnation.

Many people believe the afterlife is a Utopia, where everyone sprouts wings and becomes angelic, instantly exonerated and absolved of all their actions. They cannot accept the Spiritual Law of Cause and Effect, choosing instead to blame a personified God for the faults and inhumanity of humankind. Some argue, "there cannot be a God, for he would not allow such dreadful things to happen," forgetting the blame lies with humankind. When we all take responsibility for our personal actions and accept the far-reaching effects of that, which we set in motion, the never ending suffering will cease.

The results of our actions while in the physical shell, show in all their horror or glory, when the consciousness shakes free from the material self. Without the physical mask, our thoughts, intentions and motives, cannot be hidden from sight. Our newly arisen self is fashioned from the *true nature* of our earthly thoughts and desires. The reality a Soul gravitates to after death, differs very little from this life, for the person who refuses to be responsible, for whom they are. Our sincere prayers, are invaluable to the work of Spirit, because they help so many Souls to finally face themselves with honesty.

Chapter Eleven

Spirit Guides

We further our own Soul growth when in a spirit of fellowship, we turn back to help another. The wisdom and knowledge we have gained must be passed on. By our example, we can lead another to discover their spiritual pathway and if we wish, travel a while with them. There are many roads leading back to the Great Spirit and each of us must tread the path we choose. None are left to travel their pathway alone for our Spirit companions walk beside us.

The wonderful teachings given by a Spirit Guide speaking through an entranced Medium have been recorded in several books. These are invaluable as they speak of the life of the Soul and the Spirit world beyond this reality. Guides share their knowledge of the Soul's journey and the experiences it seeks in an effort to grow. They also tell of their efforts to lessen the fears of the dying, by supporting them with a strength that eases their passing. No one is left to die alone for many kindly Souls in Spirit surround them. The victims of tragic accidents are lifted free and nursed to an acceptance and understanding of their new state of being.

Some spoke of the progression open to every Soul and the brilliant light that shines from the Soul who attained peace and serenity during its life on earth. They tell of Spirit's united efforts to show the human race we are all 'one' for each living thing holds a spark of the Divine. This Divinity is the Spiritual Self, the Kingdom of Heaven we must seek within.

The Spiritual Self accompanies the Soul through out its experiences, patiently waiting for the Soul's realization of its connection to the Divine. When this truth is understood, it brings a greater alignment with the inner self and accesses a strength to rely upon. We are more than a physical body, we are a spiritual being, a part of the Great Spirit.

43

The Soul within this material self, came from God who gave it free will. In the expression of free will, we have forgotten our spirituality, but the Spiritual Self has never deserted us. Through every era of life on earth, there have been Great Soul's, who knew these truths and shared them in an effort to remind us of our true nature. The Nazarene showed us by example, how to live "doing unto others as we would be done by." He taught his followers a way to come to God and told them to pray to The Father in Heaven. Through his understanding of the Divinity within, he asked that we seek first the Kingdom of Heaven within ourselves.

Mahatma means *Great Soul* and Mahatma Gandhi taught by example, a nonviolent resistance to the injustices suffered by his people. His first battle was to overcome his own smaller *self.* With the strength he gained through self mastery, he fought and won freedom for the oppressed. There are Great Souls on the Earth today, who quietly go about the Father's business. Gentle people who achieve a great deal to benefit humankind. Unsung heroes and heroines whose spiritual qualities have a lasting effect on the lives of others. Their work may not be noticed or admired by others, but reward awaits them, in the reality they return to upon their death.

The quality of teaching given by such wonderful Spirit Guides as White Eagle and Silver Birch, far exceeds that of modern *channellers.* The inane and mechanical movements of communicators claiming to be extraterrestrials, ancient warriors or various arch angels are not the result of Spirit cooperation. These entities have strong egos, and make their identities and experiences known foremost. Void of higher wisdom they attach to self-promoting individuals who have a need for histrionics and drama.

A Spirit guide has overcome their personal identity and ego. They often delay their own progression in order to teach humankind a spiritual way of life that all must respond to. We should measure their worth by the quality of their statements, not by whom they claim to be.

White Eagle is a Spirit guide who spoke through the deep trance Mediumship of Grace Cooke. His work with Grace Cooke can be found in a series of books written by Ivan and Grace Cooke.

Silver Birch was the Spirit guide of Maurice Barbenell, an English journalist. The home circle formed to facilitate this phenomena, was known as the Hannah Swaffer circle. It consisted of several Fleet

Street editors and journalists, who wrote several books recording the teachings of Silver Birch.

Spirit Guides work together in cooperation in the development circle group setting. Whichever type of Mediumship is being developed, it is overseen by the circle Guide and a group of Spirit workers who follow his direction. It is a well-organized event because of this fundamental cooperation. They achieve much more, when group members add to the cooperative energy. Guides do not decide which Mediumistic ability we will develop, but with their nurturing and our commitment, all facets of Spirit communication are possible. If we are determined to develop one particular aspect of Mediumship, we form a barrier of rigid thought that interferes with our total Spiritual Unfoldment.

An acceptance of Spirit communication is now widely held by thinking people in all walks of life. Spirit's task now, is to prepare us for the after life and the Soul's continuing journey. They seek to remind us, while we are in this physical plane, there is a spiritual pathway we should be treading. The work of Spirit is not only to comfort the bereaved, with evidence of a loved one's existence, but to instill in us, as spiritual beings occupying a physical body, the realization that life is eternal. This truth should change the way we ride rough-shod over others in our materialistic greed.

With an outpouring of conscious raising energy from Spirit, the everyday mind will eventually grasp the foolishness of its ways and seek spiritual awakening. Our sins of commission and omission belong to us. We are responsible for all our wrongdoing and held accountable, before our Soul can progress further.

One of our Spirit companions may elect to guide us through a particular personal difficulty. Their qualifications come from similar experiences, when they too drank the last dregs of the cup of unhappiness. Having survived the experience, it remains as a badge of honour to be worn by their Soul. Our emotional self is often the burning ground and affairs of the heart, the scene of trial by fire.

Everyone knows the pain of separation, abandonment and betrayal of one's tender-most feelings. It is a trial through which each Soul must pass. Searing the emotions of sentiment, it builds a lasting dependence upon the core of strength within. Some spend their lifetime trying to pass this trial unscathed, destroying their sense of self in the process. Spirit companions still remain close by, supporting with love and compassion, their earthly companion's struggle. Nevertheless, they obey Spiritual Laws that compel them not to rob another of a Soul experience. When the struggle is over and self acceptance is learned, the physical self feels battered, but the emotional self has gained strength and balance. The imprisoned splendour reveals more of its strength and we know we have passed an emotional initiation, when the inner Spiritual Self tells us *"you will survive."*

Chapter Twelve

Exotic Guides

I met a man with an interesting story to tell, during a recent trip with my family to Hong Kong. He had experienced a reassuring contact with his grandfather, who had recently died in Australia. Although the grandfather was elderly, the sudden illness that led to his death, did not give them time to say goodbye.

Soon after his grandfather's death, the man had a very vivid dream where his grandfather assured him he was alive and well. He spoke of other family members in Spirit, who had passed on before him and of his pleasure, reuniting with them again. Assuring his grandson there is no death or need to say goodbye, he asked him not to be sad. Nor to feel guilty, because they had not seen each other before his passing.

Before the grandfather left, he explained how easily he had contacted his grandson in Hong Kong. China, he said, was an open doorway between the two worlds. Because of the ancient spirituality of the Chinese people, the links between this world and the world of Spirit, remain open.

Many Chinese Guides work with Spiritualist Mediums. Their wisdom and knowledge of the two realities is invaluable to Spirit communication. Often acting as master of ceremonies, they conduct the work of the development group, from corresponding upper circles, overseeing all that takes place in our unfoldment. Many deep trance Mediums work with a Chinese or Oriental Guide. As loving cooperation grows between the instrument and their control, the Guide teaches through the Medium.

In most instances of deep trance control, the Guide will perfect his thoughts to overcome the differences in language between himself and his instrument. If a Medium believes a Guide will speak with an accent, they will influence the Guide's speech patterns, although they are unaware of their interference. Nevertheless, it remains the

Medium's responsibility to control this, bleed through of personal thought. The Medium who lays aside his own personality, affectations and expectations, offers unconditional cooperation to his Spirit companions.

It is not necessary for any Spirit Guide to speak in the language or idiom of the personality they represent. Very often that, which is spoken of by the Chinese influence, originates from the minds of many Spirit colleagues. The Medium who remains conscious during the Guide's control, will be aware of their opinions influencing what is said, and can discipline their thoughts accordingly.

When witnessing deep trance control, make allowances and appreciate the difficulties involved in this rare form of Spirit communication. A useful yardstick to measure the experience, is to assess the quality and value of what is taught, rather than judging the personality who is saying it.

In my experience as a Spiritualist Medium I associate the rich colour of gold with these wonderful Chinese, spiritual teachers.

Another race plays a vital role in Mediumship. The North American Indian always takes part in the training and education of a Spiritualist Medium. They walk beside their earthly counterpart, protecting, challenging and preparing the potential Medium for the work of the Great Spirit.

Their influence begins with the individual's Spiritual Unfoldment. They encourage us to bring forth the spiritual warrior within, and overcome the earthly personality. The North American Indian lived in harmony with nature and saw the Great Spirit's handiwork in all living things. With respect for all life forms they thanked Mother Earth for her bounty. Because of their spiritual beliefs, many choose to work as emissaries between the two worlds. Despite the image Hollywood famed, of warring, violent savages, the Indians of the Americas lived closely to the earth and the Great Spirit.

In my parents' home circle, an Indian Guide spoke of his people's rapid disappearance from the earthplane. Many Indians, he said, no longer needed the earthly sojourn for their Soul's progression. They had become spiritualized and had no further need for experiences in this material world. Working from the Spirit planes, they train us to overcome the smaller self's desires for greed and acquisition. As warriors who have fought and won the war with their lower selves, they dare us to find bravery and courage within ourselves. The challenge is to become a spiritual warrior during our lifetime.

Spirits of their ancestors guided the elders in decisions concerning the welfare of the whole tribe. Sitting in a *circle* they knew how to free the individual consciousness and to speak of its experiences. Spiritual gifts of discernment, enabled each warrior to attune to the Divinity in all things. Those who despised the Indians saw this as merely a talent for tracking, not understanding their attunement with nature and their ability to be in tune with their environment.

Tribal community life was important to each child's survival. Every tribe member played a responsible part in each child's welfare. In our materialistic way of thinking, we may look upon their way of life with disdain; but in today's society, we have nothing to compare to the spirituality of these wonderful people. The colour I associate with my Indian guide is a vibrant red.

My Egyptian Guide, Atheon began my training, when my clairvoyant sight registered geometric shapes, that floated in and out of my consciousness. It was sometime before I realised his involvement. The geometric shapes led me into avenues of discovery that I did not connect with Spiritual Unfoldment. How wrong I was. I owned a very ancient dictionary and would sit for hours, leafing through the thin pages, fascinated by the original carved wood block images. The next time I held this hundred year old, leather bound book, it fell open at a page containing a lengthy discourse on Pythagoras of Samos. My love of symbolism can be traced back to this point.

With synchronicity? No, with Spirit orchestration, other information about Pythagoras came my way. All led to subjects that previously held, only a passing interest for me. My geometric imagery had by now, fused into one shape, the triangle. This was to be the calling card of my Egyptian Guide, just as the single, pine tree is the Blackfoot Indian's. The far reaching effects of this Egyptian Guide's companionship was then, beyond my understanding.

A study of Astrology, became the next step, in my training. A need to know my *self*, seemed to be my motivation for learning this complicated subject. My computer produces astrological charts within minutes today. During this period of study, there was no access to computerized astrology programs. With plenty of free time, after a recent messy divorce, I taught myself the mathematical equations

49

needed, to erect a natal chart. A new world of symbolism opened before me and all that I found, seemed familiar.

The natal birth chart is a map of the heavens at the precise moment of birth. It is a blueprint of the attributes and weaknesses of the Soul inhabiting the new physical self, and the tools available to the new personality. The planets impel, they do not compel. Our life's pathway is not carved in stone, neither can it be predicted with certainty. Interpreted symbolically, our astrological natal map reveals trends that may, or may not guide us.

For students of Mediumship, with a leaning towards symbolism, I highly recommend a study of astrological symbolism. It is a useful tool for understanding the Self. Atheon the Egyptian, has guided me through many levels of awareness, teaching me to expand my consciousness, and to enfold it once again to a more manageable size. With symbol and allegory, he encouraged a search for deeper meaning inherent in all he showed me. He gave me a sense of the brotherhood of Eternal Spirit, from which we sprang and to which we will, in time return.

My colleague, Joan had a beautiful guide, a Nun whose features overshadowed her at times. I watched her and the Nun become as one, as they walked slowly through a friend's garden. When Joan gave a public demonstration of her Mediumship, the Nun was always close by. Feeling that she had several Soul experiences as a Nun, may have helped the close alignment the Spirit Nun achieved in Joan's light trance lectures. Joan, did not just believe in reincarnation, she *knew* it to be true.

Chapter Thirteen

The Blackfoot Indian

The Spirit world has played an important part in my life. Wherever I have lived or worked, they continued their loving connection. Through chance conversations with strangers, clients or business colleagues, Spirit led me to individuals, whose spiritual gifts further enhanced my development. One of these connections was, a deep trance Medium, whose guide, gave me encouragement to face some difficult times ahead. He first spoke to me in a private sitting offered by his Medium. His words have remained deeply etched in my memory, for he spoke of a time when we were brother and sister. In a lifetime in America, we belonged together as Blackfoot Indians.

He said he had watched over me, for thousands of years and was overjoyed to have an opportunity to renew our connection. I asked him to speak in the language used then, but it did not stir any long forgotten memories.

The emotional upheaval around me at that time overshadowed the experience. I was twenty-three years old and preoccupied with a failing marriage. The Blackfoot Indian's friendship carried me through the months ahead, bolstering me, until marital matters improved. On the last occasion we spoke, he told me not to grieve so over the loss of my two Siamese cats, for very soon, life would revolve around my children, waiting to be born.

I have heard from him in unusual ways over the years since then. Never again through his Medium, but in visions of a single, tall, pine tree, a symbol of his name. Often, this was given to me by other Mediums, who were unaware of its significance. In a dream, I saw his Indian life end in death. He arose in his Spirit body, before his physical body hit the ground. Obviously, he knew how to die, for it came with such ease. Never far away, he guided and supported me through some Soul wrenching experiences. Although, I often clouded my awareness of his presence, with fear and self doubt, when the fog cleared, I knew where and when, he had walked beside me.

During a personal disappointment over a loved one's disloyalty, he stood before me. He came to comfort me, saying I had earned the last of five white feathers, but I screamed at him to keep them, for they had cost me too much. My Soul felt seared like the blade of a sword, tempered in the hottest fire. The reward of five feathers did not compensate. Much later, when in a better frame of mind, his words were easier to accept and I examined their implications. There was a different strength in me, and although I felt emotionally battered, this soon passed.

For most Mediums the burning ground is the emotional self, and invariably what should be our closest loving relationship, becomes the arena. A battle of will begins between one seeking self reliance, and one determined to destroy any Soul growth that outshines them, the lesser of the pair. All this is done in the name of love or for love's sake. We each have a worthy opponent, who if we let them, willingly reduces us to dependency.

Survival in these situations, is the best revenge, and skills developed while earning the Indian's feathers, strengthen my resolve to only follow the voice of God. Speaking to me through his ambassadors, my Spirit companions, I learned to align my will with the will of the Great Spirit. At times, this was difficult to do, but these experiences *did* strengthen facets of my Soul for the journey ahead.

The man Jesus, withstood the temptations of others who would be his masters, by relying on the inner voice of his Father God. Maybe, as human beings, we must tread a similar path before we turn to the strength of the Divinity within. Our experiences may seem harsh, but they effectively purify the Soul, so it cannot forget the experience, and inflict the same control over another. It is worth remembering, the crime is far worse, if the criminal knows better. Ignorance of the effect of our actions is understandable, but the cause still extracts a price. To deliberately inflict one's will upon another, after being subjected to the same torture, is unforgivable, for we know better.

Chapter Fourteen

Spirit's Guidance

My mother and I were sitting in our local Spiritualist Church. In my sixth month of pregnancy, I looked about ready to deliver. With her help I waddled the short distance from my parents' home to attend the Wednesday afternoon service at the church my family belonged to. Because of my size, we chose to sit in the front row, to give me more room. The visiting Medium's address was excellent and we looked forward to her demonstration of clairvoyance. The church was full that afternoon, but I was lucky, for the Medium singled me out for a message. She described my grandmother, Nan, whom she said was standing beside me, waiting to tell me something of importance. Nan wanted me to know, "One of the babies is a girl, and her name is to be Angela." My mother turned to me with a stunned look on her face and repeated the words, one of the babies, are there two?

With hindsight, I realize I had always known I was carrying twins. This was the first confirmation of an inner knowing that had not quite reached my rational mind. My only question in childbirth class, was about the birth of twins, and I surprised myself asking it. It was the 1960's, and although my natal medical care was regular, doctors puzzled over my advanced size and shape.

Our family doctor found two heart beats. He had delivered me twenty-five years before. It seemed most appropriate for him to be the doctor to find the presence of two babies. With tears in his eyes he gave me the news, yes there were indeed two babies. Sonograms were not used in the National Health Service at that time and to confirm his diagnosis, I was x-rayed! On June the first, Angela and David arrived one month prematurely. Nan's message was correct, one of the babies was a girl and we named her Angela, her Spirit chosen name. In later years, Spirit told me they came to this earth as twins, for the marriage would not have lasted long enough to produce two pregnancies.

Guides have taught and walked beside me throughout my life. I felt very alone when self-doubt clouded my awareness of their presence. Never withdrawing their love and support, they taught me a self-reliance that draws from the limitless strength within that each of us holds. Many times I gratefully bowed to their wisdom as my children grew. During a particularly harrowing time, an Oriental guide attracted my attention, and introduced himself as one who was attached to the twins. He had listened to my fears and concerns for my children and came to reassure me, that he was constantly near to guide and protect both of them. They grew in safety, watched over by Spirit, as all children are.

Spirit's presence guided them through Soul experiences, which have strengthened them into responsible adults with a strong link with Spirit. His awareness of Spirit, brought confirmation of my mother's closeness, when clairaudiently, my son David heard her whistling for him. He never knew that during my childhood, my mother constantly whistled the most complicated classical pieces. It delighted David that he was able to be so aware of his Grandmother.

At fourteen years old my mother's beautiful whistling reached the ears of a handsome young man who would, much later, ask her to marry him. He heard her when he was visiting family neighbours and asked to be introduced. They married some years later and the rest we could say, is history.

Chapter Fifteen

Guided Development

During my late twenties, my Spiritual Unfoldment continued, when I joined a Mediumship development group. My Mediumistic abilities were blossoming but were not ready yet to be used publicly. The main focus in life, was caring for my four year old twins, but weekly attendance in a circle group, kept me sane and trained me for future work with Spirit.

Another member of the circle, spoke of an Egyptian guide, she could see with me, who gave his name as Atheon. This person's development was excellent so accepting her message was easy, but the Greek sounding name bothered me. Many years later, Atheon assured me, his Egyptian name was unpronounceable, so he had made himself known by the Greek aspect of himself. Spirit Guides, will do all they can to confirm evidence given by them, even if it takes time to do so. Due to circumstances beyond my control, it would be several years before he had an opportunity to speak to me through another.

During a telephone conversation with a very gifted young Medium, she told me of an Egyptian she saw clairvoyantly. He asked her to tell me his name was Atheon. This was very evidential, as she and I had never met. She had not been part of the same development group, nor was she aware of my introduction to a new Spirit colleague many years before. The confirmation delighted me, but the mystery of the Greek name remained.

Spirit companions, find me an easier target to reach, when I am preoccupied with other tasks. One of my jealously guarded times is to read in bed, before settling to sleep. Nevertheless, as soon as my attention was absorbed in a book, another part of my consciousness, became aware of Spirit visitors. It was during one of these occasions, Atheon chose to show me the reason for his Greek name. This time my inner sight opened to reveal a wonderful Egyptian figure standing before me. With one hand he reached to remove his Egyptian headdress. In this single, simple movement, his persona changed to a handsome Greek man, with the same laughing eyes and friendly smile. The Egyptian and the Greek were two aspects of the same Soul.

His loving companionship, and spiritual teaching, led to a love of symbolism, that enriched my spiritual life in many ways. During initiation into a mystery school I saw his wonderful Egyptian figure, in full regalia, superimposed over the master's chair. He helped to keep my development within due bounds and I am grateful for the inner strength this discipline brings.

Involvement in the Spiritualist movement, years of personal development and Spiritual Unfoldment, brought opportunities to try my wings. My first public address as a fledgling Medium, loomed near and inspiration deserted me. While trying to distract myself with a Yoga magazine, this phrase caught my eye. "It is fear little brother, it is fear." Fear! What a perfect subject for a lecture.

Rules of this event, did not allow a speaker to refer to notes. The talk must be unrehearsed and Spirit inspired. Well, Spirit had inspired me with a title, and I was experiencing dreadful fear!

It was winter time and the British people had once again, to endure unscheduled power cuts, due to union disputes. As I drove to the public hall, to keep my appointment, I prayed for a power cut to happen while I stood before the audience. When my turn to speak arrived, I walked to the platform in full electric light. With shaking knees and trembling voice, I faced my audience. The title of my address is Fear, I announced. Please watch me very closely, as I am about to show you a very good example of fear. Tension eased as the sound of their laughter raised the rooms vibrations and helped me to steady myself. Strategically placed candles quickly illuminated the darkness, when, a short way into my subject, the electric company began another power cut. In soft candle light, I completed my inspired and Spirit orchestrated address.

Stage fright has never left me although it is now easier to govern. Part is humility that should be present, without humility the personality tends to rule. However, feelings of apprehension are mostly due to a change in energy, that enables us to attune to Spirit coworkers.

Chapter Sixteen

Forewarning

My Spirit colleagues have never overshadowed my free will by being forceful or demanding. Our association is one of loving awareness and compassion, patience and cooperation. Many are old friends and we have reunited, to continue working in companionship.

They are a guiding influence, for they have signposted my way and remain with me, throughout this earthly experience, often waiting patiently as my resolve, to do the Great Spirit's work faltered. All are wonderful Souls who continue to seek growth and enlightenment, fulfilling Spiritual Law by leading us to the door of our own knowledge. Each speaks of the human Soul's continuous existence and of life in the Spirit realms. When necessary, they come to prepare me, for an imminently stressful event. The following incident clearly illustrates this.

My father was in his late sixties. His health was deteriorating rapidly, and his numerous diabetic comas, kept us in a constant state of apprehension. He had gone to stay with my mother's sister in the South of England, and this gave us some relief from anxiety. During a relaxed moment watching television, my inner sight registered, on the periphery of my awareness, a small moving picture of a full sized Indian Elephant. Its progress continued, until it stood in line, with the pair of sandalled feet, standing before me.

My gaze met the eyes of an Asian Indian man dressed in soft, white, Indian khadi cloth. He was tall, with the wildest mop of dark hair I had ever seen. He said there would be news of the *man* the next day and it would not be good. Both he and the elephant, promptly disappeared. My thoughts were filled with disbelief, as my rational mind dissected the experience, I was not sure which man, the Indian referred to. Spending too much time alone, no doubt, had increased my anxiety and I was imagining things.

My aunt telephoned me in the early hours of the following morning, to say my father had been hospitalized the previous evening. He had been involved in a serious car accident and had suffered a severe stroke. He eventually died five days later. The Indian *elephant* Guide's forewarning had prepared me for the bad news. This taught me never to distrust my awakening clairvoyant sight again.

There are times when it is comforting to be reassured about a coming event, but on this occasion things got out of hand. A friend's second child was due sometime in April. No one knew on which date and my friend, whose first delivery still haunted her, dreaded the birth. She said she would feel better knowing which day the baby would arrive. As she voiced her fears, my father's voice broke into my thoughts. He told me to tell her, the baby would be born on his birthday, April 19. I had not realised he had listened to our conversation, but knew beyond a doubt, he stood close by when he spoke to me. The baby, a little girl, arrived on April 19 and my reputation as a Medium fell to the level of fortune teller. No amount of explanation from me would dispel this label. It was easier for others to believe the information came through my powers, rather than to accept, my dead father had joined in the conversation.

I have never understood, why so many people seek to consciously know their future. Could they deal with the reality of what is to come? The unrevealed consciousness holds a blueprint of several preordained incidents, that we may, or may not, succeed to in this lifetime. An Astrological birth chart, shows the attributes and qualities of the incarnating Soul. Difficult planetary aspects in the chart, give opportunities for Soul growth. However, if the aims and choices of the indwelling Soul remain dormant, ignored or overruled by the personality, goals remain unrealised during one's lifetime. Opportunities arise, but if the present personality will not take the challenge, chances are lost.

Until the individuality of inner strength takes the reins, we aimlessly follow and repeat similar patterns. A whole lifetime may be spent, avoiding the Soul's inner prompting. This delays our reunion with the Great Spirit, which is every Soul's destiny. We create our own reality and the repercussions of our present thoughts and actions, form our future. If we change our attitude, our future changes. Sometimes, our attitude is the only free will we have, and we must surrender to the Will of the Great Spirit.

Loneliness often has us settling for less, when there is no inner strength to rely upon. We seek at-one-ment with another, before forming a relationship with ourselves. When the longing for completion, turns us inwardly to alleviate our aloneness, the Soul responds and we grow in inner strength. Then we attract to us like-minded, compatible companions who have also grown in inner knowledge.

Many ill-informed people are afraid of contact with Spirit, fearing they will be told of their own, or another's impending death. Spirit will never frighten us with something we have little control over. When we gain knowledge of the smaller self and Greater Self, an understanding grows of the various levels of our being. It is my experience that we do indeed know, in the unrevealed consciousness, all that is before us. Inner preparedness, often filters through during our silent relaxed moments and we are also prepared, for future difficulties during our sleep.

During the 1960's, my mother had open heart surgery for the replacement of diseased mitral valves. Although this surgery is common place now, it was then in its infancy. The procedure was successful, but it was a harrowing time for my mother and the rest of the family. Within two years she began to deteriorate and unbeknown to me had made plans for further surgery. During my sleep, she came to warn me of her decision to have the procedure redone. I awoke hearing my own voice begging her not to. Something I failed to do, when we met the next day and she told me her news. Her incredible bravery and inner strength made me proud to be her daughter, but the months ahead were difficult for all of us.

My mother looked forward with great interest, to a new medical procedure, that involved floating a small camera in through a main artery. This enabled heart specialists to make an informed diagnosis. She talked of nothing else, excited by the prospect of watching this fascinating phenomena on a television monitor. No one knew when the procedure would take place.

On Wednesday afternoon, I walked towards her bed, in the large open ward. As our eyes met, I knew instantly, that the anticipated procedure, had not been pleasant. We did not have time to speak, for I felt her pain and fainted. As I regained consciousness I heard my mother's voice explaining, to the nurse she had called, that I suffered with my nerves! Unfortunately, my sensitivity absorbs like a sponge, the feelings and experiences of another's suffering or tale of woe. My family always consider me to be, a bit of a ninny, scared of my own shadow and I was often told, to pull myself together. When shock throws the various selves out of alignment, they do indeed need pulling together. Resenting this lack of understanding, I avoided as much as possible, tales of surgery and suffering. I have learned to govern my extreme sensitivity, so it cannot overwhelm me in quite the same way.

In the first year of my new marriage I awoke during the night very alarmed. Someone, with a badly damaged knee stood before me and I knew there was some danger ahead. My new American husband had knee surgery scheduled for the following week and I placed my fears in that direction. His ambulatory surgery passed without incident and he rested and recovered. Four days after his surgery, my daughter rang us from the Royal Masonic Hospital in London. She had emergency knee surgery, after a very bad fall some days before. She and my son kept the news from me, knowing their stepfather needed my help. The dream warning was of her fall and explained why I cried "oh no," as I awoke with a start. Now there were two loved ones with injured knees, one on either side of the Atlantic.

Spirit did warn me indirectly of another's impending death although I did not interpret the message as such. Joan, my friend and colleague, had felt unwell during the weekend. She tried to cancel plans to visit a friend but this person simply refused to take *no* for an answer. Not feeling strong enough to resist Joan allowed herself to be railroaded into keeping their arrangement. I offered to drive her there and we used my long journey home as a reason to leave early in the evening. On our way home my mother's Spirit voice joined our conversation. She told me "tell Joan she is moving into a new vibration." Joan was delighted to hear this and said "oh, I just knew my work for Spirit was changing." The following Monday morning, I learned she had died in an asthma attack during the night. Her work with Spirit did change, and she had moved into another vibration.

Joan's Mediumship was very rare and unusual. She insisted, she never saw or heard a Spirit communicator. But her detailed descriptions of deceased relatives, were recognised and accepted by the recipient of her message. With great courage and trust she attuned herself to Spirit raising her consciousness to a level of awareness far beyond the capabilities of most Mediums. On the periphery of her being she blended her perception with that of the Spirit contact. I loved and admired her and her gift and she envied my clear-sightedness.

The day after her death she stood before me in my kitchen. Not believing my eyes, I asked aloud "is that you Joan?" The reply was typical of her humour, for she retorted "you, are the one that sees and hears!" Her presence was strongly felt during her funeral, where she drew my attention to a wall plaque, carved with the words "never doubt, I am always near."

"As the physical body is the vehicle for the Soul, so is the Soul the vehicle for the Spirit."

Janet Cyford

Chapter Seventeen

Personal Experiences

My Spirit colleagues have never asked or expected me to lay aside my free will. They taught me it was God's gift to humankind. Our purpose is to exercise our own free will, until we can voluntarily surrender it, to the Will of God. We are free to willingly work with Spirit or to experience our lives in different ways. Access to their guidance helped me to navigate my own pathway through life. They counselled me to seek strength and guidance in the stillness of myself but sometimes I found this impossible to do. Trusting the inner prompting of our own Spiritual Self should be so easy. The battle lies however, with the desires of the present personality.

Once again through the vehicle of my dear aunt's wonderful gift, another guide, the Jade lady, gave me her advice. I had left my first husband, after a beating, (he called it an unfortunate slap) blackened my right eye. The bruising spread across the bridge of my nose to my left eye and I looked a sorry mess. Injuries to my neck and spine, remain today, as reminders of these unpleasant times and experiences. This particular beating could not be disguised. It showed on my face and took several weeks before the bruising completely disappeared. I, however, planned to keep it from my family.

Spirit had other ideas and my aunt telephoned me the same day, to ask was there violence around me. She had been chairing the service at the Spiritualist Church, when the visiting Medium gave her a message from Spirit, telling of my distress. After much Soul searching, I gathered my eight year old twins, the cat and the dog and left my husband. With my aunt's help, we went into hiding to give me a chance to recover safely and to begin divorce proceedings. On the first night away, as I tried to sleep, the Jade Lady's voice spoke to me through my sleeping aunt. Spirit, she said, could not tell me how to deal with the difficult problems ahead, but, she added, "no one is allowed to destroy another's Soul, so my child, do not allow yourself to be destroyed."

I asked about the effect this drama was having on the twins. She told me, they were strong Souls, who would gain further growth by their stout heartedness and she assured me, they had the right parents. A statement that gave me plenty to think about. Do we, in some instances, come together solely to give our children the correct genetic make up? Or did one or both of us fail to give enough caring and support to the marriage arrangement? This same guide, counselled me in the early days of this troubled union. I was warned then that my life would be like the road to Calvary, if I continued in the marriage. At that time, there was no doubt in my mind that I should stay and my children were born eighteen months later. I believe I made the right choice.

Our time spent in hiding with my aunt, was enriched by unseen visitors, whose presence brought a rosy pink haze, to the one room cottage we stayed in. Once again, my Spirit friends fulfilled their promise to . . never leave me comfortless.

My Spirit coworkers have never been as overbearing and coercive, as some of my earthly colleagues. It is an unforgivable sin to force our *will* upon another and a Medium learns with experience, to say "no" to overbearing personalities. For our own wellbeing, it is best to remove ourselves from their influence for stubborn people refuse to take no, for an answer. We are here on earth to fulfil our own Soul's purpose, not the purpose of another.

An outstanding Medium gave me one piece of important advice. When she was aware of my choice to work for Spirit she advised me never to allow anyone to work in my personal power. Being inexperienced the implications were beyond me. Now with hindsight it is clear I allowed this to happen and the confusion and bad health that followed were due to disregarding this excellent advice. Two Mediums can learn to cooperate with one another and receive, from a Spirit communicator, the same evidence simultaneously. However, this takes its toll if one cannot work in their own power and unconsciously draws from their colleague.

In the past, many potentially gifted Mediums have been ill-advised by others, who should have known better. The excellence of their gift has suffered through too much public exposure, too soon. By allowing ourselves to be overshadowed, we weaken our carefully forged link with Spirit and self doubt destroys our inner knowing. We receive Spirit's advice in the stillness of ourselves, when in doubt, it is the only advice to follow.

Some strange experiences also taught me to protect my awareness from others intruding thoughts. A man belonging to a mystical order, often boasted about his occult powers to anyone willing to listen. For no apparent reason he began to telephone me at the same time each Saturday morning. When he rung a third time I abruptly cut him short and replaced the telephone receiver. His pointless calls were annoying, they lacked meaning or purpose and were short on conversation.

Turning to enter my dining room after replacing the telephone receiver, I faced a full sized projected image of the man who had just telephoned me. Exploding with fear and rage I sent him on his way calling him every unpleasant name I could think of. He had used the telephone link to project a thought form of himself into a place he had never visited. Spirit assured me he meant me no harm. They allowed me to be aware of his intrusion because I had grown strong enough to deal with the experience. His curiosity about my work led him to pry into my private space. Ignoring the need for ethics and morals in his study of occultism he bothered many people with his out of body projections. Personally I have never understood someone's need to develop the ability to leave their body at will. It seems to me a gross invasion of one's privacy to be visited by these curious individuals. Psychic Peeping Toms. Their travels never take them much further than the polluted astral plane where negative thoughts and thought forms sink and remain. Much like the sediment that settles at the bottom of a bottle of fine wine.

Our consciousness can be released from the confines of the everyday mind in order to seek Spirit teaching and spiritual knowledge during deep inner attunement. This happens naturally when we sleep and most dreams are encounters the released and expanded consciousness experiences.

Thought travels along threads of love. Those strongly connected do seek each other especially while they sleep. I have seen my daughter's sleepy form standing in front of me. She and I were far apart and her motive for seeking me in her sleep state was one of love, not curiosity. Recovering from recent back surgery I clearly saw the faint image of my friend standing at the foot of my bed. She was sending me Spiritual Healing as she had promised to do. Her thoughts were so strong I could see her clairvoyantly. Another incident involved a very difficult stubborn individual who should have known better. Her interference spoilt friendships and her out of body projection into my living room was intrusive and she knew this. Tapping her forefinger against her nose she acknowledged her nosiness and disappeared much quicker than she came.

* * * * *

At a time when I was not looking for change, being quite content with my life and spiritual work, Spirit asked if I were willing to go further. Commending me for my achievements and spiritual growth, a formless Spirit, offered me further Soul experiences, that would required me to make some sacrifices. The Soul that appeared in my inner vision had evolved beyond the need for personal identity although I sensed a strong male energy. I did not question his authority, or what sacrifices were needed. Assuring me he would understand if I refused, he began to fade from my inner sight. My response surprised me for I answered immediately. "I will not be left behind." My mother's voice answered me saying "I am proud of you Jan."

Two years passed before any intimation revealed the changes and sacrifices before me. If these plans had been explicit, fear and self doubt would have prevented me from accepting. I have never regretted my decision to accept this challenge, for I gained a deeply rewarding love, and a companion to join me in my work for Spirit. This far outweighed the sacrifices I made.

Spirit teaches that we are on the earth, but not of it. Our connection to the Great Spirit must be remembered and expressed in all things. We may have something important to achieve, during our allotted time on the earth, but it is of little importance if we neglect those in our care. What we preach must be part of our own behaviour and attitude towards all living things. Gentleness expressed in kindly ways, betters the lives of our loved ones. Then, when family duties lessen, we may achieve other work for Spirit. Life is to be lived fully, with joy for each moment and lack of fear for the future. Trust is a difficult lesson to learn.

Chapter Eighteen

Time for Real Love.

Every Medium I have known, wishes for the loving companionship of a partner, who shares an interest in the work they do for Spirit. The loneliness of not being able to share these truths, with a husband or wife, is very difficult to bear. Far worse is the partnership, where envy sets out to destroy the Soul growth and Spiritual Unfoldment working with Spirit brings. Nevertheless, these experiences can be part of one's development, for they smooth the rough ashlar into shape. Then the inner self can withstand a greater weight.

In 1985, I made my first visit to America. Several weeks before, the few remaining members of my family, met for a cousin's wedding. It was to be the last time I would see my aunt, who, had played such an important part in my life. As we said our goodbyes she surprised herself by saying, "A transatlantic romance will begin because of this trip." Her Mediumistic gifts had lain unused for sometime. She laughed, clearly delighted to find they still worked. They had never failed her or us in the past and this occasion was to be no exception.

On the last week of my journey, I met my husband to be at a conference in Pennsylvania. When I returned to England, we wrote thank-you letters to each other. They crossed in the mail and arrived at the same time. He thanked me for the private reading I had given him. Mine thanked him for his company, kindness and ability to make me laugh with his zany sense of humour. Our friendship grew into love, through letters, voice tapes and transatlantic telephone calls. Eight months later we decided to take another look at each other and Al came to England to do just that. Neither of us was disappointed with what we found. After he returned to the United States, he invited me to come and stay. It was on this trip, my second to America that he asked me to marry him.

Never doubt the power of Spirit to bring two individuals together to support and love one another in this important work. With my

67

children's blessings, for this was all that mattered to me, I began a new life and a new important phase of my spiritual work . . . in America. We celebrate ten years of marriage this year. A successful marriage that works, in spite of incredible early interference and dire warnings from so-called friends. Having only our interests at heart, they pulled some mean tricks to prevent us getting together and staying together.

My husband's spiritual gifts are many and Spirit had plans for his development as a deep trance Medium. It is his reward for the support and encouragement he gave me, as my reputation as a British Spiritualist Medium, grew by word of mouth and personal recommendation.

We have healed each other's wounds, inflicted by those who should have loved us better. My children have received the fathering they missed. We thank God for the courage he gave us both, to trust ourselves and try again . . . It is the best thing we have ever done.

Chapter Nineteen

In America

My first efforts to present my work as a British Medium were rather daunting. Acquaintances of my new husband, curious to see whom he had married, arranged private sittings with me. I am eternally grateful to them, for by word of mouth, and their personal recommendations, news of my work spread. There is no better advertising.

My forte in England, had been to work with other Mediums, organizing and leading seminars, workshops and residential weekends. From all walks of life, Mediums came to these events to discuss in depth, the many aspects of Spirit communication. Sharing personal experiences of Spirit training, enabled us all, to correct bad habits and misconceptions. In order to raise the standard of Mediumship in Great Britain, Mediums were encouraged to understand their gifts and the mechanics involved, in order to successfully deliver Spirit's message.

During those years, I worked with several experienced and established Mediums, who had known me as a child. They had regularly served the Spiritualist Church my family attended.

Now I discovered the private readings I gave, were very different from those my new clients expected. I spent the first few moments of each sitting, explaining what Mediumship is and what a Medium does. Some clients looked at me with alarm, for their interest lay in future predictions or learning about their past lives. Subjects my Spirit coworkers would not deal with.

In the nineteen eighties, preoccupation with past life regression was *en vogue*. Talk shows hosted, New Age practitioners, who demonstrated their methods and beliefs. Fascinated, intrigued and very alarmed, I saw untrained exponents, regress people to other levels of their unrevealed consciousness. Others hypnotized clients to remove attached spirits supposedly entrapped in their aura. None could explain in depth exactly what they were dealing with.

My alarm stemmed from my training, for Spirit had taught me to respect and take care of the fine 'Web' that surrounds our awareness. It protects the every day conscious mind by filtering extraneous thought. When forcibly extended, by those who dabble in regression or hypnosis, the 'Web' thins and tears, placing the regressed person in danger.

Once the web is damaged the sensitivity is at the mercy of a constant barrage of lower thought vibrations and influences. These mostly originate in the lower planes of the afterlife. Using a sensible approach must surely include a reasonable understanding of human nature. If someone's moral code was of the lowest when on the earth plane it naturally follows they remain the same in the next life.

It seemed to me none of these exponents knew whom or what they were contacting. Obviously, they did not consider their methods to be dangerous or detrimental to the client's welfare. Several local people, who were regressed by a visiting practitioner, later consulted me. After her regression, a woman found she could not concentrate, especially when driving and asked me what could be wrong. Her surrounding auric energy was in an agitated state, similar to the effect severe shock has on an individual.

I find the most alarming aspect to be the lack of responsibility in those who play with forces they have little knowledge, respect or understanding of. With so little information anyone can *setup shop* as an expert in subjects they are not qualified to speak on. The same lack of responsibility lies in those who follow them.

Mystery schools throughout the ages demand an oath of secrecy before the initiate is allowed to study unseen forces. This protected the candidate from himself until he learned to approach his unfoldment with self-discipline. These subjects are not for the unsteady of mind or the emotionally disturbed, undisciplined individual. To be a reliable vehicle for Spirit's work we must first seek to know the real 'Self' and overcome the personality's need for drama. With dignity we can dispel the media's unflattering portray of occult and spiritual subjects.

A very attractive young woman, who looked bright and intelligent, disgraced herself completely on national television. Lying on a couch, she *channelled* an extraterrestrial. With mechanical movements, synchronized to her mechanical voice, she gave herself over to one of two possibilities. To a thought-form created from her own desires, or to a mischief maker in the afterlife, who enjoyed making a fool of her. Twitching and writhing she willingly vacated personal responsibility and continued the farce. Her followers extolled her talent for self-deception and a highly self-promoting, minimally accredited therapist, announced "She is someone who will go far."

With a little knowledge of many things, simple truths become ridiculous in their distortion. All aspects of New Age thought, psychic prediction and trance, now appear to be blanketed under one heading, "Channelling." While I agree we are all channels for healing and the work of Spirit, the word "Channelling" conjures up, by association of ideas, some very strange practices. What happened to the excellent American Mediums of the past? It was they who brought Mediumship and Spiritualism to Great Britain and other parts of Europe.

Each Medium's gift for Spirit communication, continues to grow and change. During the early days of my work in America, a new Spirit Guide stepped closer to me and took the reins. I am indebted to him, for as always Spirit understood the needs of my sitters. My beliefs and training were and still are, that Mediums need to give evidence of life after death. Now this was not enough, my clientele needed something more. Many who came to see me, had no close relatives who had passed into Spirit. The thought often amused me, that a sitting depended upon how many dead people my sitter knew. I opened myself to other aspects of my knowledge of Spirit, and taught of the spirituality I knew. Theory is useless, unless put into practice, and the private sitting proved to be the perfect situation to share my spiritual philosophy.

My new Spirit companion began by showing me the Soul qualities, strengths and weaknesses of the person before me. With my own spiritual knowledge I counselled my sitter into a better understanding of their inner life and the need for Spiritual Unfoldment. Many people who consulted me at that time were deeply involved with a popular training sweeping America. My knowledge of this discipline was and still is very little. Alarmed by the fragmentation showing in their surrounding auric energy, I asked for Spirit's clarification. Clairvoyantly, it appeared their sense of self had disintegrated and the energy field of most of them showed signs of inner chaos.

Apart from my husband there were no others interested in the deeper spiritual aspects of Mediumship and my homesickness included my colleagues in the Spiritualist movement. This did not last for long and I now realize it forced me to rely upon an inner strength and my Spirit companions. Soon I knew enough people to invite to a day-long workshop. Here was an opportunity to bring to workshop students, education in the mechanics of Mediumship and a chance to guide them on an inner quest for spiritual knowledge.

I was delighted with the enthusiasm Americans bring to the study of a new subject. I had heard of the support given to spiritual organisations conducting residential conferences, which always ran smoothly. All committee members pulled their weight, an attitude sorely lacking in similar organisations in England. Here people supported my approach to this complex subject and eagerly joined development groups for Spiritual Unfoldment.

At one of my workshops a student ran from guest to guest asking if they channelled! The majority of people had little idea what she meant. Unfortunately this type of approach is off-putting to the more serious student. The same person frequented channellers, seeking knowledge that could be found within herself. It is a road well travelled by those who want their psychic development packaged and microwaveable. They become esoteric shoppers, who do nothing well.

From these workshops, people joined my development groups, which I held on two evenings each week. It took time to overcome some student's preoccupation with extraterrestrials and past lives. They saw these as explanations for imagery created by Spirit coworkers. No amount of patient explanation from me matched the student's interpretation and some drifted on to fresh fields. This was excellent training for my gifts as Medium and teacher. Having no one to consult with, I turned to my Spirit friends for answers. There was certainly a great need to guide others to seek an inner spiritual life. I ploughed on dealing with spiritual teachings in a gentle diplomatic way growing along with my students.

My work strengthened and changed as I used Spirit's suggestions for a development format. This fulfilled an inner knowing that my work was to teach others to access the Spiritual Self within. Some have become excellent instruments for Spiritual Healing but most use their awareness to enrich their professional and private lives. All have found an inner strength to rely upon. Through Spirit's orchestration, seriously minded students joined my groups. Mostly, from the care-fields of medicine, therapy and education, they brought a disciplined and dedicated approach to their work with me.

Chapter Twenty

Special Moments

In a private reading for a young man, we had some extra phenomena neither of us had expected. A Spirit communicator appeared to me overdressed in mixed and ill-matched colours. It was hard to miss his yellow waistcoat patterned with a black motif, but he drew my attention to its design. He wanted to be sure he caught my eye, and had dressed up for the occasion. The sitting continued and reached its natural conclusion, and the young man left in a good mood, pleased with his experience. I encourage my sitters to tape their sessions with me and this client had brought a new, unopened cassette tape for his reading.

Returning home, he began transcribing the taped recording onto his computer and found an extra voice overlaying mine. While describing the Spirit contact's jazzy vest, another voice asks, "What, *are* you going to wear." Understandably, this young man was a little shaken and quickly returned to me for an explanation.

Replaying his tape on our stereo equipment, we all clearly heard a male voice speaking over mine. I believe Spirit orchestrated this to get the young man's attention and they succeeded. He joined one of my development groups and learned to govern his sensitivity. It no longer overwhelms him and he has become an excellent group member. He is a fine sensitive individual who recently became a medical doctor.

How did this happen? The strong thoughts of a Spirit coworker, recorded on the tape as he questioned the man's outlandish choice of clothing. In fun he asked, "What . . . are you going to wear?"

A young woman heard of my work, soon after her mother died. She and a friend, arranged to have sittings with me. The younger woman was very distraught over her mother's death and her husband and their doctor worried about her. After explaining to the young women, how I receive my information from Spirit and the type of

Mediumistic gift I have, we began the sitting. The mother quickly made her presence known and proved to be an excellent communicator. As her beloved mother gave evidential details of her life and the lives of her family, her daughter visibly strengthened. Spirit gave me time during the sitting to comfort the daughter with my knowledge of the after life. Her mother remained close by listening to me, and agreeing with what I had to say. Before the mother faded from my sight she showed me a pair of earrings she was very fond of, along with the dresser drawer they could be found in. The daughter was mystified by this piece of information and denied ever seeing her mother wear earrings.

She graciously telephoned me to confirm that the earrings had been found, where her mother had indicated. After sharing this information with her father he showed her an earlier family photograph, which showed her mother wearing the earrings at a much younger age. This sitting was an important one for her daughter and a turning point for myself. For the young women spoke of her experience to everyone who would listen, and she still does so, to this day. I am indebted to her for the people she has sent to me. Much to her amusement, I occasionally reward her with personal reading, earned with frequent flyer miles, accumulated by her many referrals.

With constant, daily use of my spiritual gifts, new methods of receiving Spirit communications developed and my work expanded. My preference was to settle my client, before leaving the room to attune myself to Spirit. Usually, my short ritual of prayer raised my awareness to include, the first of many communicators. Returning to my sitter, I then began the session by describing who was beside me. I had grown comfortable with this method and accustomed to the pattern, it worked well for me, when without warning it changed.

A friend suggested to her client that she should see me. Acting on the advice, the lady rung for an appointment. She arrived for her sitting and after the usual greetings and explanations of my work, I excused myself in order to change my level of awareness in prayer. No one was there. Only another practising Medium, can appreciate and understand my concern. I knew my band of workers would not let me down, but all I received clairvoyantly was a strange vision. Reason told me to go with this and I returned to my client.

Moving my awareness into the scene once again, I began the communication. Knowing my perspective, in the vision, was from where I laid at the bottom of a Well, or what I first thought to be a Well, I asked if my client understood what I described. "No," was the answer. I asked her if she had a Well near her home, but again, "no", was her answer. Turning to Spirit colleagues for further help, they told me to, "Stick with it, you are seeing correctly." The vision cleared and sharpened, as I focused on the circular opening above, where the faces of several men looked down to where I lay. This time, when describing what I saw clairvoyantly, my client understood.

Her dear friend had recently died, trying to save another man's life. He offered to carry an unconscious worker up from the floor of a toxic fume-filled tanker. He knew he must hold his breath. Struggling under the dead weight of the unconscious man, he finally reached the ladder's top rung, only to slip and lose his footing. Both men fell several feet to the floor of the tanker. The good Samaritan, winded by the fall, inhaled the toxic gases. Although he died several days later, his last conscious memory had been of the anxious faces peering down at him, through the circular opening far above. I came to an important realization. The event had been so real I felt as if it had happened to me. This pattern of 'sharing the same space' would continue to gather momentum as I surrendered to the process. Today, it is most acceptable and I am eternally grateful for the mind to mind blending that is achieved.

This fresh pattern of communication continued and by closely cooperating with my Spirit coworkers, I grew comfortable with their new methods. When a young mother came for a sitting, the first vision Spirit gave me was of a very healthy Ivy plant. The young woman's eyes widened in alarm as I described the Ivy plant Spirit held before me. It appears her mother had died sometime before the birth of her new granddaughter and in her memory my client had christened the child Ivy . . . her mothers given name. Now she wanted to know if her mother knew and approved of her new granddaughter's name. She assured her that she not only knew but approved. And I marvelled at the ingenuity that had created the symbolic thought picture. This new way of opening or beginning a sitting proved to be very interesting.

Some sittings are very successful and go with a swing. Others are much harder and leave me feeling drained having, figuratively waded through deep muddy water. On one occasion I stopped the sitting a short way into the session. The client before me only wanted to hear from his father with whom he had unresolved issues. If a communication is going to be difficult for someone in Spirit, my band of workers build the energy by bringing other family members to begin the communication. This was one of those occasions but the rigidity of the man before me, brought everything to a grinding halt. His refusal to accept anyone other than his father, created an antagonistic stream of thought that interfered with my reception of information from Spirit. This attitude is difficult for Spirit and Medium to work in. After several attempts to carry on, I told my sitter it was impossible for me to continue. He commended me for my honesty, when he realised I would not charge him for my time.

An earlier sitter, recommended my work to a middle-aged woman of some means, who had recently lost her husband to Cancer. Her grief overwhelmed her and she rejected everything I said, sobbing that she only wanted him back. Trying to support her through the early stages of adjustment I invited her into a weekly group. The peaceful energy would calm her and release the dead husband from some of her sorrow. I hoped he would appear to her during a group exercise, but she mostly sobbed throughout each session. After sometime, she had a change of heart and declared she could no longer afford to come because her country club fees were due. My fees had not been an issue between us and my hope is that she benefited from the group work and my time.

Having always been sentimental and emotional I am easily moved to tears by another's pain or sorrow. Surprisingly this is not the case when working with Spirit. While standing in the stream of consciousness coming from Spirit my communicator's emotions sweep over me without reducing me to tears. Thankful for this help I can continue to register their feelings without embarrassment.

Bringing evidence of a child's survival is a very emotional experience for the parent. These are the times when Spirit bolsters the energy by bringing other family members in Spirit to begin the private session. In this manner a very young girl was helped by my Spirit coworkers, to stand within my field of awareness. Rather than seeing her, I felt her presence within me. Not yet familiar with this method I continued to struggle for my usual visual image. She repeated over and over again, "Tell my mother I am okay." In error, I judged this as not very evidential. Finally repeating what she said, only after my own mother, now in Spirit, repeated the words through clenched teeth. *"Tell her, . . . her daughter is okay."*

The young mother had arrived with two friends, who waited for her in another room. As she returned to them after the sitting, they hugged her while she sobbed, "She said she was okay *that is all I wanted to hear.*" Always aware of my responsibility to repeat exactly what is given to me, I am nevertheless shaken when I almost miss something of such importance. Without Spirit's insistence, I might have brushed aside the child's message because it did not come in the usual manner. If we give our rational mind free reign, it creates pitfalls as it tends to interpret, judge or assume meaning, rather than allowing meaning to unfold naturally. In the earlier days of my work, my mother tightly held the reins, often instructing me not to embroider what Spirit gave me. The potential Medium strides forward in their development, when they learn to *give only what is given* by Spirit, during a communication.

There are no criteria for *seeing* Spirit. Very few sensitives see clearly defined images, nor do they hear on an auditory level. This may develop over time but most often it's received as a strong thought that speaks in our own inner voice. The voice I refer to is the interior one. That, which we argue with and seldom listening to, ignoring its presence and advice.

I have the utmost trust in my Spirit colleagues. However, a lack of trust in my own ability to hear and see clearly, has daunted my footsteps. It is a fault in need of constant discipline but if tempered with humility it keeps the ego from running the show. Without humility, we forget we work for the Great Spirit and not for ourselves. Without honesty, we claim success as our own and diminish the work of our Spirit colleagues.

I am continually fascinated by the methods Spirit uses to deliver a communication. There is a great deal of preparation on their part to rehearse the communicator before his or her debut. I often hear my mother's voice coaching a diffident person to think strongly of what they wish me to receive. She works very closely with me and her gentleness reassures those waiting in the wings to give evidence of themselves. In my particular gift, thought transfers from the consciousness of the Spirit contact, to my extended, attuned awareness.

The world of Spirit is intimately involved with this reality. Consciousness is everything for it survives death along with the Soul and Spiritual Self. While we remain on the earthplane we are all capable of raising our consciousness to Spirit vibrations and discovering for ourselves that life, is eternal. The secret is to use a disciplined and sensible approach. Know thy "Self" and seek personal control before Spirit control. The next question of importance should be, how should this wonderful gift be used? For the betterment of humankind or for one's own self aggrandizement.

Chapter Twenty One

The Kingdom of Animals

To lose a loved one is an emotional experience. The grief process runs its course, although we may *know* we will meet again. When a beloved pet grows old and feeble it takes great courage to put an end to its suffering. Sorrow increases with the decision to end our pet's life and lose its companionship. Our love is tested as we speak for them. I am constantly asked if our pets go to the Spirit world, and whether they remain attached to us with the same unconditional love they gave here.

Some people believe animals have no Soul. Therefore, they do not expect to be greeted by beloved pets in the afterlife. This arrogant attitude suggests human beings are superior to other creations of the Great Spirit. Spirit teaches us, the love we give our animals, helps them to evolve in Soul growth, on a spiritual pathway that parallels our own. Soul transmigration between animal and human is unnecessary. It would be detrimental to an animal's Soul progression, for what *could they learn* from man's ways? However, a few lifetimes spent as an animal would allow humankind to experience the appalling suffering so many creatures endure at the mercy of our *superior minds*.

Those who see the Great Spirit within all creatures, try to make amends for the cruelty and indifference of others. One wonders what kind of retribution awaits us as a human race, for we must surely pay for our indifference and lack of respect. We must be the voice that speaks for animals, for in their muteness they are at our mercy. Until the very helpless among us are raised in our consciousness, there will continue to be diseases that stem from our total disregard for the life force in all living things.

* * * * *

Our family pet, a female mutt of unknown origins, grew up with the twins. She had a mind of her own and lacked any discipline once she escaped from the house, which she did frequently. Her faithfulness and undying love were part of her strong character. At eighteen, she became deaf and short sighted, and we prepared ourselves to make the dreaded decision to end her life. I asked my mother in Spirit, to take her when the time came and to give her to a child I lost some years before. Bambi developed kidney failure, which made the decision for us. I held her in my arms as the veterinarian put her down. Several days passed in which grief washed over us, but Spirit found a way to let me know my prayerful request had been fulfilled.

I have practiced Hatha Yoga for many years, for the calming effect these exercises give on many levels. While relaxing between asanas during my next Yoga session, I saw the Spirit form of my dog. In the altered state of awareness Yoga brings, I watched Bambi run across the floor to where I lay. She licked my face and bounced around with the energy of a puppy. With one final glance in my direction, she ran to jump on to my Spirit daughter's lap. They had come to show me their delight in being together.

When Bambi was much younger, she lay asleep before me one evening as I watched television. At that time my clairvoyant sight intermittently perceived very clearly defined Spirit images, which I mostly dismissed as my imagination. This occasion was to be an exception. A Spirit child squatted to pat the dog's back. I noticed the little girl was neatly dressed. Her black patent shoes shone brightly against clean white socks and her hair looked freshly curled. As she reached out to pet the dog, Bambi lifted her head and looked back at her. Her tail continued to wag for sometime after the little girl disappeared. My imagination was not responsible for the dog's reaction. Within a short time I learned from Spirit this was my daughter, a child I had miscarried sometime earlier. She was cared for by my mother who dressed her so well for the visit. At the end of Bambi's life it seemed the natural thing to do, so the little girl who had grown up by now in the Spirit world, welcomed the dog as her own.

Many years later another much loved pet needed us to make the same decision and relieve her from the cancer spreading, at an alarming rate, throughout her body. Belle, the four year old Shar Pei, died one month from the date of a cancer diagnosis, her kidneys ceased working and she was very miserable. Again, I asked my mother to add Belle to the collection of family pets she has with her in Spirit.

Belle was an escape artist, who dug her way out of the garden, or ran off when we walked our dogs in the woods. Apart from her willfulness, she had adorable ways and tap-danced her little piggy feet to get my attention. The morning after she died, I saw her following the dogs downstairs. She stood in the hallway stamping her front paws, tap-dancing in her usual way. From her mouth, hung the red flea collar we had removed, before we buried her. She returned to bring me a present and to show me she was fine. Her unusual breed, a body full of wrinkles and paws very similar to pigs' trotters, made people love her without reservation. We miss her very much, but Belle is still her happy self, busy making new Spirit friends.

Animals have natural awareness of Spirit's presence and see more clearly than we do. Our pets are content to bask in the Spirit energy that builds in my place of work. It benefits them to live in this high energy and they usually live to be a great age. Alex, our red-haired Persian cat, finally died at the age of twenty-two after he carefully instructed a younger version of himself to take over his duties. Each of our pets suffered traumatic beginnings and found their way to us with the help of Spirit friends. We have given them Spiritual Healing and nursed them back to good health. All that is, except Belle whose fight with cancer was over very quickly. She too had Spiritual Healing, which can help those that suffer in this way, to be quickly released from the earthly self.

When I came to America I became co-parent of two very independent and aristocratic cats. Jinx and Alex ruled the household. They were not amused to have a female such as me in their lives nor were they ready to except my permanent presence. This showed very clearly in their combined expressions as they took their customary positions, after leaping onto the brass bed. Frozen in disbelief they looked at each other then back at me with a look that asked , who is this interloper.

Alex, a full sized, long haired, orange cat, later nicknamed 'Pot Roast' threw up in my shoes and left me presents outside the cat box. All calculated to send me back to wherever I had come from. It took sometime for him to accept me, but we finally bonded and he lived to the ripe old age of twenty two years. Jinx, a sleek black cat of considerable size had the longest tail I had ever seen. When we moved to a new house he discover the great outdoors. The fenced yard confined his adventures, he wasn't allowed beyond the gate. However, he soon devised a way to roam further. Too fat to get through the narrow space between the gate posts or to leap over, he went off his food for a few days and slimmed down enough to escape. What initiative!

Chapter Twenty Two

The Private Sitting

A private sitting, with a professional Medium is an excellent introduction to Mediumship. High quality, proficient Mediumship needs no advertising. When a Medium's work is beneficial to those who experience a private sitting, their personal recommendations bring additional appointment from other folk. By word of mouth and with Spirit's orchestration, people find their way to the Medium. Details of the Medium's work are sometimes taken, tucked away and forgotten, until circumstances bring an urgent need to make personal contact with a loved one in Spirit.

A young woman accepted the business card of a Medium, whom her friend highly recommended. Many months passed when a close relative died, leaving the young woman desolate with grief. Remembering the information given by her friend, she made an appointment to see the Medium. She received good survival evidence of the relative and other family members who had passed into Spirit. The divine hand is in all things and one may wonder whether Spirit knew of her future need for comfort.

Less urgent need can decide a person to arrange a private sitting. However, it soon becomes apparent their loved one in Spirit has instigated the idea and impressed the living relative, to make an appointment. Spirit's reasons are not always obvious, but they often delay a sitting until more suitable conditions arise. After transition into Spirit, some newly arrived Souls need time to adjust to their new state of being. Therefore, they may be unable to give positive evidence of their presence through a Medium, until sometime later. But this is not always so, for, many strong-minded individuals return during a private sitting, having passed into Spirit, as recently as the previous week!

Each sitting is an experiment in mind to mind rapport, dependant upon the Medium's elevated consciousness and degree of attunement to Spirit. Bands of Spirit coworkers train alongside each Medium. In unison, they work as a team with their earthly instrument. Dependable cooperation is essential on both sides of the veil. This prevents the proceedings from becoming, a haphazard event lacking in purpose or direction. Each Spirit communicator receives help to transmit their thoughts in a manner conducive to the Medium's sensitivity. Team members carefully organize every facet of information, and, can sometimes be heard instructing communicators to create in thought, an image of themselves *as they were when still in the physical body.*

The process of projecting this image to the Medium's mind, is rarely appreciated by the sitter or those with little understanding of Spirit communication. A Spirit contact who overcomes this difficult task does so by clarity of thought. Now, the Medium must discern the thought picture and relay a clear description of their impressions to the sitter.

The Spirit trained Medium does not attune to the sitter's auric field of energy. If their training has been and still is, guided by Spirit, the Medium will be aware of the origin of their information. By first seeking a Spirit communicator, authentic Mediumship conveys information from that source. The sensitive who can only perceive on a psychic level, discerns information from their client's energy. They do not rely upon a Spirit contact for information. This can be a pitfall for the potential Medium until they realize, all Spirit forms glow with an inner light that comes from their Soul. To some degree so do their projected thoughts. Information perceived on a mundane psychic level is lacking any such illumination.

When making an appointment for a private sitting, the client must refrain from giving *any* information other than their name. It is unnecessary to give details of their personal life or whom they wish to hear from during the sitting. Information given by the client detracts from the validity of survival evidence given by Spirit, and the Medium's honesty and integrity is left in doubt. A Medium seeks to raise their awareness beyond the rational, everyday mind, but if inexperienced, they can still be influenced by prior knowledge, willingly supplied by the sitter.

As an example, the Medium may question an impression of, *brother in Spirit,* if having learned minutes before that the sitter's father died recently, and they *only want to hear from him.* The more experienced sensitive learns how to deal with this by briefly educating each sitter as to the mechanics involved.

Mediumistic sensitivity is the instrument used by Spirit for communication between both realities. It is not an easy process. Spirit colleagues compare it to, using a typewriter that is floating in deep water. The association between Medium and Spirit coworker, is one of loving cooperation. The ill-informed believe a Medium can contact whomever the sitter wishes to hear from and this is just not so. We cannot summon the dead in any way, shape or form, for we understand, respect and are subject to, the Spiritual Laws governing this phenomenon.

Sitters must be advised, when making an appointment that the Medium cannot guarantee who will communicate to give evidence of themselves during the sitting. As the appointed time approaches, the sitter should prayerfully ask their conception of God, for an opportunity to hear from those they love. In this manner the sitter places their requests before God when seeking the comfort of personal Spirit contact. Without fail their prayers, if reasonable, are fulfilled.

The Medium's task is to relay survival evidence according to the quality of their Mediumistic gift. Deciding what constitutes evidence of their loved one's survival, is the sitter's prerogative. For some people, it is a recognizable description of a loved one, now in Spirit, which contains several identifying features or characteristics. For another, it will be trivial information that other family members confirm later. For a recently widowed lady, it was confirmation of her husband's presence on his birthday. In an effort to convince her he was nearby, he described her thoughts and feelings as she had strolled around his much loved garden.

A son returned in a private sitting, with flowers for his mother, something he had *always done* on his pay day. Another sitter will dismiss a detailed description of a loved one, because hair colour or height was not *exactly* correct. Others find evidence in the fact that the one in Spirit *somehow knows* of their difficulties, and gives detailed information of the sitter's recent personal struggles. Because death does not sever ties of love, it naturally follows, a loved one would draw near to support those they love, just as they did before their death.

Some sitter's expectations cannot be fulfilled in the way they would like them to be. Many only want details of their past lives, or verification of guides previously given through a channeller. If the Medium does not receive information confirming these things, the sitter is disappointed. A Medium's task is to comfort the bereaved with evidence of the Soul's survival beyond death. They deal with facts that are verifiable. Past lives cannot be proven or verified therefore, this type of information is not part of a Medium's task during a private sitting. The continuous existence of the human Soul, is a Spiritual Law and the Medium is free to believe in reincarnation. Nevertheless, it is a strange fact of human nature that those constantly seeking knowledge of past life experiences, often do so for less than spiritual reasons. It may be wiser to question oneself as to why this information is necessary.

Genuine personal experiences of the Soul's continuous existence, privately revealed to us by Spirit, come when it is pertinent to our present growth. Because these individual experiences are so valid to us, we have no need to seek further confirmation. Along with the experience, comes inner knowing and we understand, that it is, but another aspect of our Soul that lived the previous life.

Spirit Guides make their presence known to us, in many intimate ways over the course of our life. On a deeper level of consciousness, we know them. During our sleep we may be trained by them. Sitting for Mediumship development, enables the awareness to expand sufficiently, to perceive the first of many guides who will teach us when we genuinely seek Spiritual Unfoldment.

Our guides will not confirm incorrect information, however, they will lead us to those who can help us develop a greater awareness of them. Guides that appear in a private sitting, do so to confirm the *sitter's previous awareness* of them. It is foolish to place our trust in a Guide given to us by another sensitive until *we* have a personal awareness of them, or knowledge of their purpose.

It is essential for the Medium, to give a short explanation of his or her Mediumship, and what the sitter may expect from the session. If there is sudden entrancement, it is very alarming and bewildering to a sitter with no experience of trance Mediumship. An explanation of how the Medium receives information from Spirit, gives the sitter an idea of the mechanics involved.

A sitter's response to detailed information, given by the Medium, should be a simple "Yes, I understand" or "No, I do not understand." A strong vocal reply strengthens the Spirit contact, and prevents the Medium labouring too long over one point. If the Medium's description of a Spirit contact is unrecognised by the sitter, they must say so. This allows the Medium to ask the Spirit communicator for further information. Questioning the sitter is not good Mediumship, and will be seen as fishing for information.

By carefully observing my work as a Spiritualist Medium, I have come to realize we must give the discarnate Spirit, time to relay their carefully rehearsed information. The communicator's flow of thought is easily interrupted, if we assume to know their meaning. This will result in poor evidence, that is full of confusing detail, all due to the Medium's lack of personal control.

If the communicator's thoughts arrive too rapidly, the Medium must ask her coworkers to adjust the speed of delivery. The simple, but friendly, "slow down" will tell the one in Spirit his thoughts are arriving in a jumbled fashion. Nevertheless we appreciate the positive mind, over the slow thinker, whose musings become difficult to follow.

The mental Medium often receives superimposed images of *two people,* both eager to get through. If the presence of two communicators is unrecognised by the sensitive, the description given will baffle the sitter. When the Medium detects the presence of two Spirit contacts, one will step back, when asked, waiting patiently until the Medium is ready to focus on them. However, coworkers will not be aware of the problem until the Medium makes them aware of the overshadowing. Then, they willingly make the adjustments needed.

A sitter can ruin a private sitting with fixed expectations. Some will not accept personal messages from anyone, other than, the person they wish to hear from. Another may decide that nothing will convince them of a loved one's continuous existence unless they speak of a certain matter, only known by both client and communicator. This creates a difficult atmosphere for Spirit and the Medium to work in. It creates an antagonistic stream of thought that bars successful reception of Spirit communication. A lady who had a private reading with me dismissed all evidence of her father because he apologised for his overbearing attitude towards her and her family when he was alive. Her reasoning was, he never apologised for his behaviour when he was alive, so it couldn't possibly be him. Although other information confirmed it was indeed, her father. It is not unusual for a loved one to apologize for their behaviour towards others. Part of the Soul's progression is to review their life and the effect their actions had on those they touched upon in their life.

Reception can also be spoilt by a sitter's negative attitude to a Spirit messenger. Thought becomes distorted by atmospheric interference in a manner similar to a bad telephone connection. In this situation, it is best for the Medium to stop the sitting, explaining why it is impossible for them to continue. Thankfully this does not happen very often.

One seemingly intelligent young woman, arrived with a photograph of a male actor currently appearing in a highly successful musical. She held the picture closely to her, to prevent my seeing his face. Her actions were wasted on me, as my information comes from Spirit, not from my sitter or their personal possessions. During the sitting, her loved ones gave evidence of their presence, which she reluctantly accepted, but no one mentioned the photograph, or her romantic life. When the sitting was over, curiosity got the better of me and I asked what she was holding. It appears, she met this stage artist after one of his performances. He signed a publicity photograph of himself and it was this that she brought to the sitting. The actor had greeted her as warmly as he had greeted other fans. Blinded by his friendliness and her own feelings, she consulted a psychic who assured her of his undying love, devotion and their future together. She arranged a private sitting with me, hoping for further confirmation.

Nothing I said could convince her, the psychic had fed back as a prediction, her own strong attraction and dreams of a future relationship with the actor. It is these strong emotions that the untrained psychic attunes too, and delivers as actual fact to the one consulting them. Alas, we are all free to believe what we chose to believe and we do indeed, create our own reality.

The sitter must feel comfortable and be reassured if they are nervous. Many have preconceived ideas, inflamed by the media, of what to expect when consulting a Medium. They are pleasantly surprised to find that nothing frightening happens and the self respecting Medium looks as normal as they do. Only small talk is appropriate until the Medium attunes to Spirit in silent prayer. Trying to put a suspicious individual at ease recently, I asked if she had ever consulted a Medium before. Her sharp reply riled me. "No" she said "I didn't believe I would ever be so foolish". We parted on good terms, but her suspicious attitude challenged me. With experience we learn to shield our heightened sensitivity from suggestions that we have gleaned our information by reading body language or by trick questions. Or worse still, we have spent our precious time and energy researching the client. We don't have to convince anyone or prove anything. But we must always act with dignity, humility, honesty and self respect. In this manner we help to dispel the media's representation of Mediumship. This client was determined not to reveal anything that might give herself away. "Do you recognize this communicator from my description?" brought forth a blank stare. "Do you understand", received the same response. A simple yes or no is all that is required. It's common courtesy to give our voice in response to the efforts made by a nervous loved one in Spirit.

Some message Mediums do not receive names from a Spirit communicator. Occasionally, they are heard phonetically and repeated in that way. Impressions of a grandmother may be clear, but, which side of the family she belongs to, unfolds as the communication continues. If the sitter suggests a name, this interrupts the flow of thought from the Spirit communicator. Not all sensitive's work on an auditory level, but they should be prepared to give any names they receive in thought, from Spirit. Strangely enough, a name often registers clearly upon the mind, when the one in Spirit refers to someone, other than themselves.

I received help from my grandmother in Spirit, when a communicator had difficulty letting me know who she was. The image of my loved one was disconcerting, until I realised she *stood in* for my client's grandmother. This helped my communicator whose character proved to be very similar to my grandmother's. Both were called Nan!

Clear contact occurs when images and impressions flow unimpeded, by the Medium's or the sitter's thoughts. No two Mediums receive information from Spirit in quite the same way. However, with dedication and involvement in their work, gifts continue to grow and improve.

It is unnecessary for the sitter to bring a list of written question to the private sitting. If they insist, the Medium must refuse to alter the method of their work to suit the sitter. This may be acceptable in a psychic reading, but the Medium's training is to reach for a Spirit contact who relates to the sitter. It is helpful to the sitter and the Medium if the session is tape recorded. This gives a true record that the sitter can refer to later. Some find deeper meaning when re-listening to the recording. Other living relatives often confirm information unrecognised by the client during their session.

Because the world of Spirit, is intimately involved with our material world, loved ones in Spirit know of the sitter's needs and reasons for having a private sitting. Whom they want to hear from and answers they seek, are spoken of by the Spirit communicators when giving evidence of themselves. It is far more evidential, if a Spirit contact speaks of these things. This should leave no doubt in the sitter's mind that the information given to the Medium originates from a Spirit source, not from the sitter's mind.

Personal experience has proved, once the Medium has greeted the sitter, Spirit communication can take place without the sitter being in the room. Soul survival evidence received by the Medium, will come unimpeded by the sitter's expectations. However, there is a lack of warmth in this arrangement and nothing proved other than, information does not come by the Medium's *trick questions*. Sitter and Spirit communicator, benefit from the love that builds in this time of reunion. Grief heals with Spirit messages from our loved ones, and old wounds close forever when forgiveness and understanding is asked for and given.

The Medium acts professionally, by being ready to begin a private sitting on time. Spirit coworkers prepare suitable conditions, and the Medium anticipates these preparations, as her sensitivity heightens, when the appointed time draws near. Sitters who casually arrive *after* the prearranged time, are ignorant of these preparations and the effect tardiness has on the Medium. A careless attitude disregards the Medium's work, which is often seen as, light entertainment. By the very nature of the energy used in good Mediumship, very few appointments can be filled during one day, and late arrivals disrupt more than a carefully arranged schedule.

The Medium will welcome positive feedback and confirmation, after the sitting and before the sitter leaves. Some will telephone later when other family members confirm some information unknown to the sitter. Unfortunately, a few believe the Medium is always readily available, and willing to continue the communication with further evidence sometime later. They are disappointed when the contents of their sitting is not fresh and clear in the Medium's mind. A self disciplined worker for Spirit will firmly close the doors of perception, as the sitter leaves. Because of the nature of this work, it is essential to the sensitive's mental health to forget the contents of each sitting. In all Spirit communication they stand within a stream of consciousness that holds the communicator's strong emotion and the sometimes uncontrollable grief of the loved one who remains behind. Controlling my overwhelming emotional ability to empathize with another's grief, proved to be an easy task with Spirit's help. In a public demonstration of clairvoyance an emotional reunion between recipient and communicator left me tearless and in control of myself. To my amazement I felt their strong emotions bounce over me, even though they registered on my sensitivity. I am extremely grateful for the help Spirit gives me in these emotional moments.

The content of a sitting can be very draining to the Medium whose emotional or mental selves have become depleted. The nervous system strengthens with Spirit's help, but overwork and tiredness will eventually take its toll. A recent series of private sittings were for mothers whose sons had died in various tragic circumstances. As a parent, one identifies with their grief, but as a Medium, we must rise above any personal emotion to function efficiently during the private sitting. A precious child's death, is senseless at any age. The comfort communication brings, does not lessen the loss, but eases the grief of a parent who believes they will never see their child again.

Evidence from these young men, accidentally killed, in different circumstances, had one thing in common. Each spoke of relatives in Spirit, helping them at the moment of death. Were these relatives forewarned, but unable to prevent the accident, because each son's lifetime was completed?

We can only speculate, if indeed, there is any accidental deaths. If there is an appointed time to come into this life and a time to leave, an accidental death may be the manner in which we return to Spirit. We can take comfort from the knowledge, that a better reality awaits the Soul, when freed from the restrictions of a dense material physical self.

Spirit Guides speak of the divine hand being in all things. Ambassadors of the Great Spirit are present, in the worst of situations, ready to lift the Soul free of its earthly body at the time of its passing.

Chapter Twenty Three

Public Mediumship

Public demonstrations of Mediumship usually commence with a *Spirit inspired* address. According to the Medium's ability, this may be delivered, while he or she is in one of several stages of attunement. Inspirational speaking, is a rare facet of Mediumship that is often overlooked. It needs the same degree of cooperation with Spirit that every other facet of Mediumship requires. In its perfection, it provides wonderful opportunities for highly evolved Spirit teachers to expound on deeper spiritual subjects.

It demands a meeting of minds between Spirit Guides and their earthly instrument the Medium, but, it does not depend upon the Medium's knowledge. The subject matter originates from one or several Spirit minds blending their thoughts in such a way, they fleetingly lay upon the Medium's mind. In the deeper stages of attunement, the Medium's personal opinions are overshadowed and they often learn from the subject matter they deliver. This enables Spirit teachings to be delivered unimpeded by the speaker's physical mind. Through close cooperation and trusted familiarity, the Medium gives voice to the carefully measured, rapidly delivered, thoughts of their Spirit inspirer.

Inspirational speaking can be found in other walks of life. If the speaker is in service to humankind, their public speaking contains a depth that is lacking in the carefully rehearsed speech maker. The Spiritual Laws in effect are the same for all who reach for creative inspiration. As the consciousness strives for new ways to express itself, it naturally attracts Spirit minds of the same ilk. Through the law of attraction, like minded individuals in the spirit world are drawn to those who speak of spiritual matters.

Regardless of individual expertise, trusting this process can be difficult without firstly acknowledging the potential of expanded consciousness. Relinquishing all but personal discipline when speaking publicly, allows Spirit minds to fashion the subject, in a way that is relevant to those who come to learn. Inspirational speakers aware of Spirit's participation, realize the same lecture, delivered to different audiences, can vary considerably.

A demonstration of the Medium's Clairvoyant gift follows and members of the audience or congregation, receive Spirit communications. Messages from the world of Spirit, fulfil the purpose of Mediumship. The Spirit contact, strives to give evidential information, via the Medium to establish his or her Soul survival, beyond the transition of death.

If the premises, where the public meeting takes place, are only used for spiritual teaching, the atmosphere remains light and harmonious. However, if the meeting-place has other events, social gatherings, union committees, etc., a heavy atmosphere remains. These conditions are difficult for the Medium and Spirit to work in. For the demonstration, to be informative and educational, Spirit workers help the Medium, to overcome the negative energy, by replacing it with harmony. In the Spiritualist Church service, hymns are sung. There is no better way to raise our vibrational rate than by prayer and singing.

Spirit Guides speak of their difficulties, providing clear communications in disharmonious conditions. To achieve a blending of consciousness, they must lower their vibrational frequency to meet the Medium's elevated awareness. When the atmosphere is tense or inharmonious, Spirit compares the experience to, entering a densely smoke filled room. Spirit workers are greatly helped by a positive, open-minded attitude from the audience and the manner in which the demonstration of Mediumship is presented to the public.

In a public meeting, the Medium is often aware of dominant thoughts from certain members of the audience. These usually originate from strong-minded individuals who *want* a message and set out to draw the Medium in their direction. Some people have other agendas and attempt to prove that Mediums are merely mind-readers, easily influenced by the strength of the sender's thought.

Spirit coworkers do their best to protect the Medium from being pulled off track. Interference can break into the stream of communication, in the same way a crossed telephone line will. With training and experience, the Medium learns to recognize where the thought originates and avoids being drawn into this pitfall. If however, they are unable to deal efficiently with these obstructions, they become very drained when working in public.

My colleague Joan, invited me to work with her when she conducted a workshop in the College of Psychic Studies in London, some years ago. This was good experience for me. It also provide an opportunity to learn the difficult lesson of rising above the strong thoughts of a determined audience member. An American, who bragged of his mind control training, put up an unfair fight to draw my mind in his direction. It took some effort on my part to mentally construct a wall as a division between us. The rapidity with which this dividing line grew surprised me, as I had no recollection of being taught how to do this. Spirit colleagues cheered me on in this learning experience. My efforts were most successful and once this invisible wall was in place I was unaware of any further attempts from his direction. Some months passed and the occasion and the man were long forgotten. One evening while reading in bed and to my utter amazement his face clearly formed above the pages of my book. Needless to say I sent him on his way. It certainly was a lesson in the power of thought. A course in ethics should be mandatory with this mind control training.

When a demonstration of clairvoyance or lecture on spiritual matters is arranged, the event organizers should create an atmosphere of peaceful tranquillity. The audience responds to this and harmony builds quickly. A brief introduction to the Medium's work informs the audience of what to expect. An explanation of how a Medium's work differs from the Psychics, educates the audience in the mechanics of Spirit communication.

When a Medium describes a Spirit communicator to someone in the audience, it is essential for them to hear a reply. A simple "yes, I know who this is" or "I do not recognize the description," will do. Nodding or shaking the head passes unnoticed, but a strong vocal reply reaches the Medium, the Spirit contact and other members of the audience. The sound of the recipient's voice strengthens the link between both vibrations.

Members of the audience, are asked not to give unnecessary information when spoken to, as this muddles the clarity of thought from Spirit to Medium. Trivial details are sometimes very evidential to the recipient, and we are taught to relay information exactly as given. The recipient, by giving unwanted details, preempts information that could prove the Spirit communicator's identity.

A difficulty, inexperienced Mediums have to overcome, is locating the person in the audience who connects with the Spirit contact. Some Mediums see a Spirit light hovering over one person. Following Spirits direction, a method of recognition can be arranged that works for both Spirit and Medium. It was always a difficult moment for me but by keeping my gaze out of focus, one face in the congregation would suddenly appear in clearer detail. Simultaneously, my awareness registered a Spirit form or pictorial image. It is essential, to pinpoint the person destined for a message from Spirit. If we are firm in our selection, people seated near the recipient, cannot claim the message for themselves.

In a public demonstration, or the private sitting, the Medium must repeat exactly what they receive from Spirit, with one important exception. If the Spirit communicator uses unpleasant, unnecessarily blunt or rude language we are not obliged to repeat what we hear. This rarely happens and is usually full of humour, but we must ask them to rephrase their remarks, or refuse to repeat their tactless words. A mother-in-law in Spirit, spoke very bluntly as she pointed to her daughter's husband in the congregation. They were old enemies who antagonized each other for many years before her death. She spoke of him as humourless, miserable and sour. He, however, did not have the opportunity of retaliating, for I edited her words before speaking to him.

Determined to get through to me she created in thought, a strong image of herself, as she looked before she died. This is an excellent example of the power of positive thought, always welcomed in Spirit communication.

Her son-in-law recognised her from my description, and grinned when I spoke of her continuing disapproval of his ways. Nothing had change between them. She had been in Spirit for sometime and was still exasperated, for in her opinion, he had not mellowed with age.

His future reunion with mother-in-law, can only be imagined, for not only ties of love bind us to another. So does hatred and animosity, however, these block our Soul progression, until love settles old battles amicably.

Contrary to popular opinion, a Medium is not constantly open to Spirit communication. An attunement through prayer opens the doors of awareness allowing the consciousness to extend safely. Our awareness must be closed and shielded after a demonstration of Spirit contact, so the sensitive can function normally once more. If this closure is constantly neglected the Medium's gift suffers and great strain is placed upon their emotional and mental selves.

Heightened consciousness blends with thought and feelings, of the Spirit form standing within the Medium's field of sensitivity. The closest blending of energies produces the clearest images, but the Medium over-simplifies a complicated process, when she casually speaks of seeing and hearing. Images record upon refined awareness with the speed of the camera shutter. Height, age and build are *felt* with threads of sensitivity and we describe a *perceived impression* of a Spirit form. Their earthly experience of physical pain, *briefly* registers on our material self. There is a sharing of energies and space as the two frequencies blend

To restore peace of mind, loved one's often share their last conscious memories to assure us they did not suffer. Many do not wish to speak in great detail of their last days on earth, especially if these were difficult times for the family. When someone struggled through a lengthy, painful illness, they wish to comfort us with the knowledge, that death was the easiest part of dying.

Many Souls want to reassure those who grieve for them, that they are not alone in Spirit. They tell of loved ones who met them, when they came to full consciousness in a new state of being. Some say they thought they were dreaming when they saw family members close by.

Others need time to adjust to their new surroundings. If they feared death because of rigid religious beliefs, the dream state continues, until the consciousness forms its own conclusions. Many find themselves in hospital surroundings where they are nursed, until strength and balance is regained. This helps the exhausted Soul to recover from the after-effects of a long illness. They no longer have a physical body, but the consciousness, along with the Soul and Spiritual Self survives death.

Those with strong minds and positive attitudes, reflect the same characteristics when they communicate with firm, clear and precise thoughts. Similarly, if uncommunicative when on the earthplane, they remain the same in Spirit and the Medium has difficulty receiving their thoughts.

The drug addict or alcoholic who is unable to overcome their addiction while still on earth, faces the same cravings when in Spirit. The far reaching effects of drug or alcohol addiction can be seen clairvoyantly, in the addict returning to give evidence of themselves. Addiction taints the Soul and dulls the consciousness, and much work must be done to overcome this, once they realize they are no longer alive. Those who bravely try to overcome their addictions, while still in the physical body, avoid many self-imposed problems in the afterlife. Accepting personal responsibility for their own actions, is more difficult to do once the addict vacates the earthly self.

Nevertheless, all are accepted into the loving arms of Spirit, where multitudes work to leave no one comfortless. These wonderful Souls do not judge or condemn those whose lives were difficult to bear. One who ends their life in suicide, is not left alone in the darkness of their consciousness, but held and comforted, by those who understand their struggle. Spirit asks for our understanding to be given in prayers and good thoughts for their recovery.

A Medium's work continues to change and improve, for with constant use, spiritual gifts grow and new methods are added. With great trust in Spirit, subtle improvements weave naturally into one's work hardly noticed. I look upon them as my employers, for they bring only those who will benefit from my strongly forged link with Spirit. The person who can hardly bear the loss of a loved one, feels the burden of grief lifted, when that Soul returns to say they are well and happy. The purpose of this work is fulfilled, when the bereaved find comfort through personal evidence of the Soul's survival beyond the transition we call death.

People ask why Spirit communicators do not give names and addresses. This would certainly simplify the Medium's work, if the information was received correctly. One Medium insisted upon this from each Spirit form that stood beside her. Unfortunately, this was all she received, and some communicators were never verified. Another Medium, gave stunning evidence with names and addresses, but accusations claimed information came from the church register.

There are no greater critics of a Medium's work than our earthly colleagues.

My own Mediumship is one of extreme sensitivity to a Spirit communicator's presence. It is very rare for me to hear names but when I do they are usually correct. Sometimes names are called out from the periphery of my awareness, and originate from folk in Spirit who have nothing to do with the communication I am giving. So great is the need for more 'telephones' like me that once my doors of awareness are opened a queue forms. Each waiting for an opportunity to make themselves known.

Personally, names have never impressed me as very evidential. I have watched undisciplined Mediumship struggling with common names, every member of the congregation could place in their family, or by acquaintance. The Medium hears the name of George, but cannot place whom George wants to speak to. Six people insist, without any confirming evidence, that he belongs to them. Matters deteriorate further, as the Medium is pulled in all directions. It is far better to leave the contents of a communication in the hands of the one who is struggling to make themselves known.

In Great Britain a Medium's public work is mainly in Spiritualist Churches, where religious services create wonderful energies for the work of Medium and Spirit. Organ music and familiar hymns sung by the congregation, raise the vibrational frequency of all present and the church becomes an open doorway between this world and the next. The service is similar to any other religious worship, for all go to God in prayer. The resident or visiting Medium gives an inspirational address. Unlike other church sermons, this address is unrehearsed, but inspired by Spirit. If the Medium has a trance control, a change in speech, phraseology and demeanour occurs as the trance state begins. Spiritual teaching given in this manner comes from the trust and cooperation between Medium and Spirit. This was evident in the ease with which, my deeply entranced aunt moved, with eyes closed, across the platform.

In the Lyceum Spiritualist Church my family belonged to in London, passages from, "The Aquarian Gospel of Jesus Christ," were chosen for each Sunday Evening Service. A common thread connected reading and inspirational address, although different people were responsible for these choices. A demonstration of clairvoyance by the resident or visiting Medium, then followed.

The most amazing clairvoyance, given by the Spiritualist Church's resident Medium drew large audiences during and after the war years. This particular sensitive was my aunt whose Spirit controls gave messages from loved ones in Spirit who connected to family members in the congregation. Evidence of the Soul's survival after death comforted many who had lost sons, husbands, and sometimes whole families during Hitler's reign of terror. Exceptional Mediumship from many more dedicated Mediums flourished during this time and the years following the war in Europe. Their standard of Mediumship was far superior in comparison to today's *channellers*.

* * * * *

The public needs educating in the mechanics of Spirit communication. It should be obvious to even the uninformed, that the attitude of the public audience or private sitter, contributes to the success or failure of a Spirit communication. Television journalists present opposing opinions to controversial subjects like Mediumship. A psychologist is invited to explain the limited mind and its delusions. The fundamentalist, armed with his specially edited Holy Bible, and intimate knowledge of Satan, dismisses Spirit communication as the work of the devil.

The Spiritualist religion, of which Spirit communication is an integral part, does not dilute its spiritual teachings with intimate knowledge of the devil. This seems to be the fundamentalist's forte. All Mediums who strongly advocate the teachings of Spirit, do however, view the self-serving egos of humankind to be a devilish threat to our collective progression as human beings. We do not, therefore, give the devil, or those who speak so intimately of him, any credence or credibility. Nevertheless we view the epitome of evil to be, the impinging of one's personal will power upon another. This too, seems to be the fundamentalist fanatic's forte.

Illusionists make foolish claims by dismissing all Mediums as frauds, whose only talent is for *mind reading.* A televised demonstration of Spirit communication through Mediumship, fettered by this lack of harmony, is bound to be poor. Until the television producer, protects the Spiritualist Medium from the fanatical fringe, all efforts to present a balanced demonstration of a deeply spiritual subject, will be a waste of time.

Audiences holding strongly opposing opinions, create barriers that are detrimental to clear Spirit communication. Studio lights, cameras and the confusing cross currants of production, are not conducive to the peaceful energy needed by the Medium or their Spirit coworkers. Presenters, ignorant of the nature of Spirit's work, have been seen interrupting the flow of message Mediumship, by demanding confirmation of information, given to members of the audience. Good Mediumship needs harmonious energy and pleasant conditions, in order to function efficiently. It is a fascinating subject, but television talk shows do not do it justice. Mediums seeking this type of publicity, should think before placing Spirit colleagues in the difficult position of convincing the public at large that the Spirit world exists. Greater Souls than they, have refused to prove themselves to satisfy the curious.

The Medium who feels compelled to stand in the spotlight of the talk show, must not expect miracles. If they are uneducated in the mechanics of their particular gift, they cannot defend themselves, or Spirit from the misconceptions of the fanatic or the uninformed.

The accusations that Mediumship is merely mind reading, a technique easily demonstrated by any stage magician, should be addressed. All Mediums would wholeheartedly agree, that we attune to the minds of discarnate individuals. In prayer, we open our awareness to a vibrational frequency, compatible to our Mediumistic development. *Mind to mind,* we receive strong thoughts from the consciousness of a Spirit communicator. We use our trained ability to discern their presence and the clear thoughts they wish to impart to us. Thank God, we are mostly protected from the undisciplined thoughts of our earthly companions and are unable to read their minds. I have discovered that some acquaintances are wary of my abilities believing that I am able to read their minds at will. Little do than know that at times I have difficulty reading or knowing my own mind!

Spirit has never turned away from honest investigation and has cooperated with many fine minds, seeking proof and explanation. To expose a sensitive and Spirit coworkers to biased public opinion, may be good television, but it puts Mediumship back in the dark ages. Fortune telling, psychic prediction, even witchcraft is not subjected, by the talk show host, to suspicion and opposing opinions. However, the Medium who sees and speaks with the dead, is smeared with superstition and met with outrage.

"All the answers lie within.
Have courage to begin the Inner Journey."

Janet Cyford

Chapter Twenty Four

As a Spiritualist Medium

Many Spirit companions, contributed to my Spiritual Unfoldment and training as a Spiritualist Medium. By placing myself in the hands of these wonderful Souls, my continuing development is, and always has been, closely monitored by a higher intelligence than any earthly one. They have always encouraged me to teach from my own experiences. To speak of Spirit's constant presence in our lives, and the spiritual teachings that can guide us as human beings.

My allegiance is to God, the Great Spirit and to Spiritual Laws that are eternal. Therefore, my credentials as a Spiritualist Medium come from Spirit. Not from membership in large organisations, where human egos rule and the inspired purpose for uniting to do the Great Spirit's work, is buried and long forgotten, under the weight of those seeking positions of importance.

Speaking with the authority of inner knowledge, I share in these pages what I have learned of the world of Spirit and the life of the indwelling Soul. Throughout my life, Spirit helped me to face and pass through, situations that polished facets of my Soul. With difficulty I came to realize my connection to God was within myself. This understanding did not come from sudden enlightenment, reached by daily meditation. But, through taking part in life bravely, with as much courage as I could muster. When one begins to teach from experience, a pattern of personal unfoldment emerges. With the clarity of hindsight the road travelled shows very little deviation from my Soul's intention to serve.

Personal Spirit Guides, showed me there are two forms of development, one of the Soul and the other of the Spirit. One develops only the psychic faculty, but the unfoldment of the other brings growth to the Soul. They taught me the importance of an inner life and how to centre myself in the Spiritual Self, the inner sanctum. Our Spiritual Self must be stirred before we can access the imprisoned splendour within. Once we accept this, the outward search for spiritual knowledge ceases and the richness of the inner connection unfolds. Spirit led me to experiences, which helped me understand the potential inherent in our consciousness. Showing me how as human beings, we use very little conscious awareness to function in this robe of flesh. Much, much more remains untapped, unused, wasted.

Once we find a method suitable to us, we can extend the consciousness and glimpse a little of its outreaches. It can indeed, reach to and access, vast pools of knowledge. Knowledge that is constantly fed by streams of consciousness, from great minds of the past, present and future. When the physical body dies, the Spiritual Self, the Soul and the consciousness remain. It is these aspects of our being, that continues to exist in the afterlife.

Spirit teaches that there is nothing new in this earthly experience. All New Age thought is but ancient knowledge, embraced and discarded many times before. They caution us to avoid ancient teachings presented with new twists and gimmicks, for they are of little use, unless they lead to discovery and knowledge of the Greater Self. The lower or smaller self and its material desires, must come under the discipline of self-mastery before spirituality can be truly understood.

It is the evolving Soul, who functions from its inner knowledge, that raises the level of spirituality on the earth plane. Many such Souls are on earth today and they act from an inner spiritual strength that has access to real knowledge. Spiritual Laws of Attraction, draw them to like-minded individuals. These connections may be few and far between nevertheless strong, unbreakable bonds are forged and remembered.

Unfortunately, the path the evolving Soul treads is a lonely one, for they are outnumbered by all who cannot rise above their materialism. The materialists chooses to function only in the personality; they are easily recognised by their actions, for they ride roughshod over the sensitive Souls who stand with one foot in both worlds. With no thought or respect for others, the materialist measures success by the distance between humble beginnings and present material achievements. They are unaware of their emptiness. The Great Spirit, judges us on the joy and happiness we bring to peoples' lives, not by our material wealth and the society we mixed in.

To teach from what one knows to be true is invaluable. Personal experiences have been of benefit to the many students, who have studied with me in America. In weekly development groups, they find a sensible approach to simple spiritual truths. By providing a safe environment, students learn to open their awareness and consciously control its extension. They use the safest route into altered states of consciousness and are shown a safe way to close their awareness again.

Knowing there to be, a different purpose for my training and Spirit's teaching, my spiritual work in America, has not been to train Mediums for public or private work. Following an inner guidance, my strong link with Spirit is now used to help all students seeking Spiritual Unfoldment, to do so under Spirit's personal guidance.

We have reached a stage in human experience when people desire direct and personal knowledge of their inherent Divinity. Being no longer content to learn the nature of spirituality second hand, students seek direct inner knowledge of their connection to God by beginning the inner journey.

My students have forged their own strong links with Spirit, which have enriched their personal and professional lives. This has added new dimensions to their chosen careers in health care, legal and educational fields and enriched the talents of artists in the visual and performing arts. Spirit Guides who teach from their wisdom are the finest teachers and it is into their hands we must place ourselves, when seeking personal development and Spiritual Unfoldment.

"The world of Spirit is intimately involved with our own."

Janet Cyford

Chapter Twenty Five

The Ring of Chairs
The Mediumship Development Group

The development circle group, is the foundation upon which good Mediumship stands and Spirit contact depends. True Mediumship cannot be safely developed alone. Neither is it learned by attending lectures, gaining certification or reading do-it-yourself books. Study is invaluable but theory alone does not produce the earthly instrument necessary for Spirit communication.

Real development begins in earnest with a commitment to regular attendance in a well-run circle group. In this safe environment the potential Medium can learn to cooperate with Spirit operators, who teach them to open the awareness in a manner that protects the precious nervous system from overload! Spirit's training and guidance helps each student 'to work at' the impressions and images they receive.

The purpose of all types of Mediumship and Spirit contact, is to prove life after death is a reality. The Medium registers the presence of a Spirit communicator and information received from this source, establishes who they are and what they wish to say. The well-trained Medium, who has a strong link with Spirit, can relay evidential facts of survival with personal messages from the deceased. Knowledge of the Soul's survival after death comforts the bereaved and eases their loss.

A lack of commitment and dedication to the work of Spirit has brought a decline in the standard of Mediumship. Many potentially gifted Mediums, remain satisfied with very little personal development and fortune telling now takes precedence, over the true teachings of Spirit. A renewed interest in forming and attending a development group, would educate and raise the standard of Mediumship beyond the New Age fringe of psychic practitioners.

The development of Mediumship, must come under the guidance of Spirit advisers, it cannot be learned by reading of others' experiences and adopting them as our own. However natural one's gift may be we must first learn to govern our sensitivity, so it does not dominate our lives. Being unable to close the doors of perception at will, is a pitfall for many who embark on an undisciplined approach to their development. To be at the mercy of a constant input of information, lays an enormous stress upon the nervous system and plays havoc with the mentality. Mediumship is not for the unsteady of mind, or for the overblown ego. To work safely as an instrument for Spirit communication, we must learn to protect the delicately balanced nervous system, by first seeking to know and understand the *Self*.

The burden of distress, caused by emotional, mental or physical abuse, can precipitate the sudden onset of visions and voices. Unfortunately, many are diagnosed with mental problems, when in fact, severe shock has blown wide the doors of perception. This permanently damages the protective web surrounding the consciousness, leaving one emotionally unstable, and at the mercy of heightened sensitivity.

It is essential to create a safe environment in the development circle, for the gift of Mediumship to flourish. The awakening ability to perceive on other levels, can leave the potential Medium with many problems if they attempt to sit alone. Finding a competent teacher to train with, can be difficult. So many Mediums have not the slightest idea how their gift works and could not train another. This leaves us in a sorry state of affairs as the development of Mediumship remains one of the most important tools of the modern world that lacks suitable training. Without knowledge of the mechanics involved in Spirit contact, the Medium is at the mercy of the sceptic's criticism. Not understanding how their gift works, they cannot defend this valuable work from ridicule.

* * * * *

The movement of energy in the development circle is clockwise. A ring of closed energy forms, when we join with others and sit in a *Ring of Chairs*. Our development is also circular in its unfoldment. Feeling we have reached the point of knowing all we can know, we suddenly find ourselves back at the beginning ready to start again.

Sitting in a development circle, does not bestow instant spirituality. Neither are Mediumistic abilities, an indication of a highly evolved Soul. But if spiritual unfoldment accompanies the development of the Medium's gifts the quality of communication and Spirit teaching is excellent.

The group that is inspired by and can follow Spirit directives soon finds an elevate quality of development in each student. The first task in our spiritual unfoldment is to seek the presence of the indwelling Spiritual Self. Each of us is a spiritual being manifesting for the time being, in a physical body. Our Spiritual Self has accompanied our Soul through its many experiences and constantly strives to remind us of our Soul's purpose. It is a spark of the Divine, the Kingdom of Heaven inherent in every living thing. We must experience the power of the inner Spiritual Self, by allowing it to direct our lives into avenues of unselfish service to others. Then, we can claim to be unfolding spiritually.

It is the gentle, kind, self-disciplined individual, who respects all human beings and every expression of the Great Spirit, that is walking in the light of the Soul. In all aspects of Spiritual Unfoldment we must be willing to align our personal will, with the Will of God. Then our inner core of strength can guide us.

During the last decade, my work for Spirit has drawn many students from the visual and performing arts, to professionals in legal, health and educational fields. They have joined weekly groups for personal development and have enriched their lives with the unfolding spiritual power, discovered within themselves. For many students, this has become the absolute focus of their lives as it led them to their own conception of God and added to their personal belief system.

Some have experienced a paradigm shift, that allowed them to forge a stronger link with Spirit. Quickening the Soul to a greater understanding of its potential and adding another dimension to chosen careers. By exercising spiritual awareness daily, we can uplift the sick and dying, recognize the spiritual hunger in those that seek counselling and gain greater insight into another's suffering. Group members in the health professions, soon became aware of the presence of Spirit workers, in their daily interaction with patients. Many are comforting the dying, through an awareness of the patient's loved ones, no longer living, who gather to help the Soul make its transition. They have eased the overwhelming fears of those facing death, by sharing personal knowledge of the continuing existence of the Soul and its consciousness beyond death. Patients, dealing with the terminal prognosis of AIDS or Cancer, are helped and comforted with the knowledge and understanding that death is not the end.

Chapter Twenty Six

Forming a Development Group

The perfect development group, consists of like-minded individuals, joining together to do the work of Spirit. Each member is supportive and all delight in one another's success. Those who are competitive have lost interest and moved on to other subjects. Others, who imagined there was a set pattern to their progress, have discovered this unique work is tailored by Spirit, to their particular needs. Course one, two or three do not exist in the circle development group and each persons growth cannot be compared to another's. No course work or home work is required, but a greater sense of personal awareness is soon apparent.

Essential to our unfoldment is the slow but steady strengthening of the nervous system. A highly charged emotional self can delay clarity of inner seeing. When the emotions are steadied with self mastery they become our friends and not our masters. Until strong links are forged between student and Spirit coworkers it is essential to keep one's development to the regular circle group meeting. In the early stages constantly reading of spiritual matters can place undue strain upon the inner unfoldment. In their eagerness to understand all there is to know, some group members begin to read all they can on this subject. This does not bring the effect they desire, but rather the opposite one of overtiredness and an inability to sleep or think clearly.

This work relies on cooperation. Cooperation creates the harmony essential for Spirit contact and provides a safe environment for all to work in. Each group member contributes to the conditions of the circle.

Gathering a few minutes before the appointed time, everyone takes their regular places in the *Ring of Chairs*. Loving awareness begins to grow and camaraderie adds to the tangible energy, which has accumulated over many years in the circle group room. Visitors

111

coming to stay over, find they sleep well and leave our home refreshed by the Spirit power that fills the house.

For those wishing to develop their awakening sensitivity further there remains the problem of how to begin. The sensible way would be among like-minded companions, who appreciate the need for discipline, structure and a sane approach to a very complex subject. Several compatible friends, who are willing to commit to a weekly session for development, would be ideal.

Forming a group for Mediumistic and Spiritual Unfoldment, is rather daunting to those who have no personal awareness of Spirit's presence. There are many folk who will not form or lead a group, without a practising Medium. This is a self-defeating attitude for it disregards the ability of Spirit to guide us by inner inspiration. In the early days of modern Mediumship, people sat together without a fully developed Medium and under Spirit's guidance, all types of phenomena occurred.

Chapter Twenty Seven

The Group Leader

The most important component of the group is a sensible leader. It is not necessary for him or her to have clairvoyant sight, but they must be willing to act upon their inner prompting. This is how Spirit inspires us; we just have to listen and follow through on their inspirations. A leader needs to be strong enough to take the reins and have reached some degree of self-discipline. A practical person with common sense, is far better than one whose knowledge comes from books they have digested. Their responsibilities include, starting and finishing the group session on time and allocating a reasonable amount of time to each sitter's contribution to the circle group work.

It is necessary for the leader to have a flexible mind. A rigid approach that insists upon doing things as they have been done in the past, excludes all possibilities for Spirit guidance. Times have changed and development has changed along with the times. Group leaders must remind members, to keep to the point of gathering together and not allow the group to become a social event, where some come to chat or moan about their lives. It is also unwise to let a group, meeting regularly for Spiritual Unfoldment and Mediumistic development, to deteriorate into personal therapy sessions. Groups meeting for in-depth therapy need qualified therapists.

Leaders must insist, members arrive with minutes to spare, before the designated starting time. This enables the work to begin smoothly without interruption. Late comers are warned, not to disturb the group once it has begun. As the awareness extends, the sensitivity is easily shocked by sudden noise. The telephone or door bell will disrupt the tranquillity. Therefore, group members must arrive with time to prepare themselves for the circle work. Allowing members to linger after the group session is unwise. Rehashing experiences, reopens the carefully closed doors of awareness, leaving the sensitivity vulnerable to extraneous influences. A leader will feel very drained if expected to discuss personal problems or matters concerning the group. Because of the sensitive nature of this work, sharp criticism of another's development during the circle group is unwise. Occasionally, use one session to air opinions and give and receive constructive advice or criticism.

Chapter Twenty Eight

Aims and Intention

Newcomers should be informed, before their acceptance, of the guide lines upon which the group is formed. With clearly defined goals it is easier for the appointed group leader to gently pull on the reins when things get out of hand. In time, it will be apparent Spirit are leading newcomers to the group. Until then trial and error are wonderful teachers and one learns who is, and who is not, suitable for this work.

Harmony is essential to Spirit's work. If someone is disruptive, ask them to leave. When there is an undercurrent of jealousy or dislike it erodes the harmony needed for our work with Spirit. If two or more members are vying for leadership this results in a disharmony that needs resolving before progress can continue. Members of the circle, experience a variety of feelings and emotions, as a bond of love and companionship establishes a link between circle members and their unseen visitors. Courtesy, support and one's full attention are qualities expected from each group member. There is nothing more disconcerting than cross-talking. It is rude and unkind. Fidgeting and constantly shifting position, is also disturbing and disrespectful to other group members.

The size of the group is important, and it should not exceed eight people. Six, including the group leader, is a manageable size to begin. As the group grows with success and the leader feels confident of Spirit's inspiration, others may join. Commitment to attend regularly is essential. Once the group is formed Spirit workers commit their time to working with us. When we are casual about attending regularly the continuity of development suffers. With only five or six members, several cancellations reduce the group size to very few. It is also essential to begin and end the group on time.

In the early stages sit for only an hour. This can extend to one and half hours as the leader becomes more experienced. Dividing the hour into fifteen minute segments, the leader can section the group's work, organizing it into a structure that creates harmony and safety.

Each member needs a clear understanding of the group's aims, intentions and reasons for gathering together. Whether the consensus is for Spiritual Unfoldment for all or to support one person's Mediumistic development, everyone should be in accord agreeing to the groups intention. If the group wishes to meet for passive meditation, then so be it. This is an excellent method for quieting the self on all levels. I can only share my experiences of development groups whose primary purpose is to forge personal links with the world of Spirit and the Spiritual Self within. It has not been my experience that this comes through passive meditation alone. When we seek contact with Spirit the mind needs to be alert and very much alive to all thoughts impressed upon the mirror of the mind.

If the intention is to forge individual links with Spirit, then keep to that aim. Those with interests in extraterrestrial contact should form a group of their own and take advice from those they seek to contact. Spirit coworkers *do not work* with us under this guise and it is detrimental to the group when one or two individuals wish for, or seek this connection. It is the leader's function to squash those things that do not come under Spirit's guidance by discouraging all leanings in that direction.

The probability of extraterrestrial life and the possibility of human experiences is not disputed. What must be emphatically stated is, UFO's or men from Mars, have nothing to do with our work with Spirit. The territory under exploration *lies within*. This should be of great importance to all who embark on self-discovery and Spiritual Unfoldment through the development of Mediumship. Forget outer space, gather courage to begin the inner journey.

I have crossed swords with many potential students who wished to impress me with their knowledge of occultism. Attempting to gain control of hidden occult powers, is *incomparable* to working within

116

Spirit power. While the former creates power for power's sake, the latter reveals the need for perfect harmonious cooperation. Some believe in the power of magical forces, but have difficulty accepting the reality of Spirit communication. It is important however, to differentiate between what occult power evokes and the power, built by Spirit, for communication between the earthplane and the afterlife.

Elemental and nature spirits, willingly work in cooperation with evolved Spirit companions. These forces of nature, respond to gentle kindness in the same manner as they do for the gardener with a green thumb. In Mediumship, their help is invaluable if physical phenomena, such as table tilting, levitation, or transfiguration develops. However, it is unnecessary for us to understand their function for them to be effective.

Under Spirit's direction I learned of these energies *after* forging personal links with Spirit Guides. It was they who led me in safety, to experiences that taught me the difference between spiritual and occult energy. It may be of interest to those, recoiling at mention of the occult, to realize the word means . . . hidden. So, it is but hidden or secret knowledge being sought. My advice to those interested in occult knowledge, is to join one of the many mystery schools available, where expert training can be found.

"Seek the serenity and unconditional love of the Spiritual Self within."

Janet Cyford

Chapter Twenty Nine

The Spiritual Self

There needs to be a quieting of the various 'selves' before the group begins. Most students arrive after a full day's work and a long drive. Anxiety and tensions reflect as agitation in the energy surrounding the physical body. A period of silence allows the energy to settle and everyone to prepare for their work. When working in altered states of awareness, we must begin by creating an interior silence in the peaceful environment of the Ring of Chairs. Each group member learns to switch the focus of their consciousness away from their material concerns in order to make an inner attunement. This allows the auric energy to settle into a stillness free from the agitation and activity of our personal lives.

An inner journey that centres us within the Spiritual Self is the place to begin. Self awareness through spiritual awareness must be the goal and what better place to start than by discovering the Divinity within. Each of us is a Spiritual being, manifesting for the time being, in a physical body. Our Spiritual Self has accompanied our Soul through its many experiences, and constantly strives to remind the personality, of our Soul's purpose. It is a spark of the Divine, the Kingdom of Heaven, inherent in every living thing.

The first journey of the consciousness requires a surrendering of the smaller *self*. It can be done by leaving our material concerns outside of our awareness. When we switch the focus of our consciousness away from our material reality, it is free to travel into the presence of the Spiritual Self, the Divinity within. This inward journey is a centring of one's selves. By creating an interior silence the various selves come into alignment, allowing us to access the core of strength within. Once the indwelling Spiritual Self responds, it speaks to us in symbols and allegory. (For some have seen an image of a perfectly formed double-edged sword. This symbolic image, among other things, depicts the strength and power of the spark of Divinity within.)

With thoughts focused on the inner journey, we enter the inner sanctum of the Spiritual Self. We tread upon our own sacred ground and experience the Divinity's embrace of unconditional love. The Spiritual Self has stirred and responded to our awakening and consciousness rediscovers our true nature. For we are all, of Spirit. This inner splendour, renews us with peaceful tranquillity, poise and serenity of mind. From this state of consciousness, the group becomes as one mind, in unity of thought. Now we join hands in our *Ring of Chairs* and begin our work with prayer.

Chapter Thirty

Prayer

All work with Spirit must begin with prayer. Prayer naturally changes our level of awareness and vibrational frequency by lifting our thoughts towards the Godhead. There is no better method of opening our awareness than with prayer. It enfolds us and the group in the light of the Great Spirit. Nothing can pass through this enfolding light *unless* it is of the same calibre as those who join in prayer. The auric field of energy, which settled during our inner journey, now spreads outwardly blending with persons sitting either side of us. Its light reflects the degree of attunement each student makes.

If we open our awareness to inspirational thoughts from Spirit, the prayer flows with natural energy. Whether one individual gives the prayer each week, is a matter of choice. If alternated between members difficulties can arise. The person whose turn it is to open in prayer, either rehearses beforehand, or is unexpectedly called out of town that week!

Spirit suggested a method for opening circle work in prayer, which proved to be very useful. More than the spoken word occurs when using this collective prayer. By joining hands in *The Ring of Chairs* a continuation of power passes on as each person contributes one or two sentences. Moving in a clockwise direction, the theme of the prayer continues and Spirit light secures the circle. The group leader can choose who shall begin the prayer.

It is essential the prayer is not restarted half way round the group. Although this sounds obvious, it happens frequently. Breaking the prayer's continuity defeats the purpose of the exercise, which is to raise the awareness of all who are present. The opening prayer is to open the group's level of consciousness, so each persons contribution of a sentence of two must be to open the group. Likewise the closing prayer is the place to give grateful thanks to all who have joined us from those unseen realms, and to bring each group member back to their driving home consciousness.

Some group members pray for protection, but when questioned are never sure from whom they need protecting. Like attracts like, if our aspirations are of the highest then like-minded spiritual teachers are attracted to the quality of light emanating from the circle group. A quality created and maintained by the endeavours of all who join in prayer. We mostly need protection from ourselves and our ego. I have never feared Spirit friends but have often feared humankind and their machinations.

Chapter Thirty One

Absent Healing

After the group circle is opened and raised in prayer, the work begins with our second level of attunement and we receive personal Spiritual Healing. This God-create energy, revitalizes the physical self and strengthens the nervous system, protecting it from undue strain during our development. With the help of the healing power, the emotional self and the mind, balance and stabilize. As our colleagues in Spirit, direct this power to each layer of ourselves it assists us to make other gear changes, in our level of consciousness. Each student experiences the nature of the healing energy. Some see rays of vibrating colour, as the healing power embraces them.

If there are suitable members with healing potential cooperation begins with Healing Guides, wishing to develop a partnership for Spiritual Healing. First, the potential healer learns that the healing power comes from God and cannot be created by humankind. It *is* the God energy, which comes only from the God source. It is not "psychic" healing, which uses the healer's energy but a power that originates in the highest.

Before healing can be received, Spirit adjusts the power's vibrational frequency to the patient's needs. Spiritual Healing is only as effective as the healer's attunement to the Great Spirit's power and his or her ability, to take thought directives from Healing Guides. Only through perfect cooperation can the healing power flow through the earthly healer to the patient.

Spiritual Healing is not Faith Healing. Faith is not necessary for the healing power to work. Neither is healing dependent upon extensive training in Therapeutic Touch, Energy Balancing, Reiki nor Mariel. These methods are beneficial *only if* the practitioner attunes to the healing power originating in the Great Spirit. Special hand movements or various touching methods, copied from other healers are superfluous and irritating to the patient's sensitivity. Spiritual

Healer's need only act upon their guide's directives. They ask for the simplest of methods to be used that are not in anyway theatrical. The healer should place their hands within the patient's field of energy, or gently on the patient's head, if they are so directed by Spirit.

Nor is it necessary to attune to the person requiring healing. Merely standing or sitting near the patient enables healing to take place. However, without the healer's attunement to Spirit, both healer and patient will suffer a depletion of energy.

It might be beneficial to discuss each group member's understanding of healing energies. If several people believe they are using their own energy to heal they are at variance with Spirit's teaching.

We can benefit from the calm energy of trees, blossoming flowers and the earth, but the healing power being discussed here, is not drawn from the earthplane. It is only accessed by attunement to Spirit. Healing Guides must use us as a vessel to ground the power. A lightening rod, a conduit, a clear channel in the form of an earthly companion is needed to focus the healing energies.

The person who overcomes negative personality traits becomes a better vehicle for Spiritual Healing. Nevertheless, our desire to be a healer should be honestly examined. Humility and compassion for all suffering are paramount, for with these qualities the natural healer . . . heals. Attunement through prayer prepares us as vehicles for the Great Spirit's healing power. Immediate results are not often evident, but continue to trust the process. The physical body is the last vehicle to express disease; therefore, Spirit will direct Spiritual Healing to the level where disharmony began.

Many times the cause lies within the emotional self where, a state of being 'at variance,' rages war and conflict. If the various 'selves' are out of alignment with the Soul's purpose, the resulting disharmony cripples and disables. When in a weakened state of debilitation, germs and viruses gain a foothold. Knowledge of physiology or biology is not a prerequisite for the healing power to be effective.

Animals also benefit from absent healing, they too can be placed by name in the healing power. Spiritual Healer's find animals also respond to hands on healing. The same rules apply, for they too, are creatures of the Great Spirit. Animals deserve our compassion, respect and apology, as an act of contrition for the appalling suffering humankind has inflicted on them.

Healing Circle groups form to send healing to the sick and to develop healing potential in group members. Healing is also effective when sent to nature and mother earth, places of war and strife, nations and their leaders. In the spirit of brotherhood, all mentioned are drawn nearer to their understanding of the Great Spirit and healing begins. Healing thoughts for the well-being of all life, accumulate by attraction and grow in substance and momentum.

The time allotted for healing in a group sitting for personal spiritual unfoldment, can be extended for longer periods in a group formed as a Healing Circle.

Having received personal Spiritual Healing in our circle group setting, we must now give to others. Concentrating on the ever increasing healing power manifesting in the group setting, students place friends, family and acquaintances by name in the healing power. Many keep a journal, in which they write the names of those in need of continued healing. They mentally hold this in the healing light.

A great reservoir of healing power is constantly replenish with our thoughts and healing prayers, which must be free from all personal desires. This can be drawn upon by those who need strength and courage. In humility we are aware we cannot do this alone, but in cooperation with Healing Guides, our thoughts join the multitudes in Spirit who direct this God force.

Placing people by name in the healing power is called Absent Healing; it is remarkably effective although the person is far away. Focusing on the person's spoken name also helps our inner perception to unfold. Students may receive impressions, of the person named, from Spirit Healing Guides. Others may develop a healing gift while sitting in a development group. Healers trained by Spirit learn how to attune to their Spirit counterparts. Using the same cooperation needed for Spirit communication they learn to surrender to Spirit's directive. This enables them to be a pure, clear conduit. The same format suggested for development circle groups will assist the work of a Healing Circle group.

The power of healing prayer accomplishes a great deal, but our prayers must be free from personal desires. If we pray for anything other than strength and courage for the one who suffers, we are usurping the Will of God and interfering with an individual Soul's purpose. We must constantly remember, our desired outcome *may not be* the best choice for the Soul passing through a difficult experience.

This is particularly difficult to accept when a child is suffering. It can help, if we remind ourselves that prayers for their strength and courage, add to the loving care of healers in Spirit, who support and comfort them.

Healing power, can help the terminally ill to surrender and peacefully let go. The very special person inhabiting a diseased or crippled body, is often a highly evolved Soul, supplying others with opportunities to gain patience, compassion and understanding. These qualities, become part of our Soul, once experienced in great depth. We can only guess, which choices a Soul makes. However, we must consider the Soul growth gained by each person associated with the sufferer. In our absent healing, we pray for strength and courage to be available to all who struggle and all who support them.

Chapter Thirty Two

Expanding the Consciousness

After a period of personal and absent healing, students take part in exercises designed to strengthen their individual link with Spirit. During this time of personal development the quality of energy differs from the intensity of the healing power. It should be remembered however, that our consciousness is under our control at all times. When we sense, the presence of a Spirit companion close by the awareness has begun its extension. The student is always free to withdraw from the experience, for it is an exercise in cooperation with Spirit. Not, as some believe, possession by a discarnate mind.

The surface of the mind when stilled by passive silence, reflects images of strong thought directed by Spirit colleagues. If we acknowledge them with our inner voice they respond by giving clearer images or further information. Until we respond positively to their presence, they do not know we are aware of themAcknowledging the visual thought impressions, creates a stronger *mind to mind* connection with our Spirit coworkers.

When sitting for Spiritual Unfoldment and the development of Mediumship, do not hold the mind in a state of passive inactivity. Allowing the consciousness to sink into a stupor is not the aim. When the inner dialogue of the rational mind subsides, our consciousness expands unfettered by mundane, unrelated thought. Free from interruption the mind becomes receptively alert, actively alive and poised in its awareness. A stilled pool of water clearly reflects that, which is above it. In the same manner, Spirit reflects thought images for us to receive upon the stilled surface of our mind.

Exercises that strengthen our links with Spirit colleagues are essential to the development of Mediumship. It is a method of Mediumistic training that forms a foundation for Spirit communication. Gentle sensory expansion hones the perception without straining the nervous system. Forced psychic development however,

127

thins the protective web surrounding the consciousness. Serious students avoid courses promising instant psychic awareness, knowing development comes only through slow but steady progress. Even with a natural gift, it is essential to learn to govern the sensitivity in the safety of the development group setting.

As awareness expands and blends in harmony with others in the developing group, students may experience unfamiliar sensations. A temperature change is sometimes felt that chills the lower legs and feet, while the air above remains warm. This is quite common when the healing power is replaced to facilitate an exercise for personal development.

We must remind ourselves we are experiencing vibrations utilized by Spirit operators. In an altered state of awareness, students begin to register the presence of different energies merging with their own. Experiencing feelings of enlargement in the fingers or hands, signals the expansion of our consciousness. This sensation plagued my childhood until my development as a Medium began in earnest. Then the once familiar feelings were recognised and understood.

These sensations are common, but often mistaken for out of body projections. Consciousness, is expanding beyond its normal limitations, and we feel the physical body's density as our vibrations rise. Familiarity with the process, leaves us undisturbed when a higher frequency joins ours and Spirit steps, into our extended field of energy. If however, this becomes distressing, it is easily altered by asking for Spirit's help. Plain, drinking water supplied to each group sitter, is also a reviver and quickly changes the level of awareness.

My experience is that several Spirit coworker's draw near to each sitter. As a band, their collective energy forms a mantle. Concentrated, in alignment to our spinal energy, it surrounds us from our left to right sides, gently holding us in a half circle of intensely focused Spirit energy. It is a useful exercise to discern this process as it takes place. Students may find it easier to watch changes occurring around other group members.

Chapter Thirty Three

Conscious Journeying

With Spirit inspiration, and under the group leader's direction, a journey of the consciousness can begin. The everyday mind needs to be transcended in order to function fully in extended perception. A focal point for the awareness to focus on is useful, perhaps a mist that slowly clears to reveal Spirit imagery. However, we must be ready to move on from this point when our personal Spirit companions guide us further. In this manner, the stimulated consciousness becomes actively involved, in the unfolding Spirit imagery.

If the leader acts upon his own inspiration he can describe to the group, images that Spirit places in his mind. In his mind's eye he may see a corridor before him. Large wooden doors line the passageway. Speaking aloud of what he perceives, he leads the group into the scene. Their task is to choose a door to enter. Once a door opens in response to their choice, they cross the threshold and enter the room beyond where a Spirit communicator awaits them. At this juncture, the group leader leaves his students to experience the *Spirit orchestrated* exercise.

This method of guidance, stimulates our brain-waves and thought processes are set in motion. Once thought is activated Spirit operators place imagery, pertinent to each student, into the mechanism of extended sight. It is of little benefit to our development, if we allow the mind to wander into other avenues of thought. Each group member's task is to follow the exercise. Later, comparing experiences members find they walked through similar scenes that differ considerably in detail. The importance of imagery is manifold, for it actively involves each of us to seek personal meaning.

It is important the leader does not give lengthy descriptions of the scene in his mind's eye. He must not include every minute detail. Describing a green armchair, confuses the student who sees, in their inner sight a blue, straight backed chair. It seems an unimportant point, but many students struggle with the concept that, *it is Spirit* placing imagery upon our mind's reflective mirror. With experience the leader's choice of words will free group members to see images, Spirit prepares for them personally. For example, asking the group to find themselves in a holy place, where a Spirit guide awaits them, gives choice to which type of holy place Spirit wishes them to see. Whereas, leading the group into a church of *their* choice, limits Spirit imagery.

Remember, it is the heightened consciousness that travels into the received or described imagery. These methods do not promote or require, an out of body experience, where a projection of oneself invades the privacy of another. A difference that must be experienced to be understood.

An exercise of this type is invaluable to early development. By sign posting the way, Spirit slowly stretches the extended awareness at a pace suitable to each individual. When the mind freely follows the images given, momentum gathers and Spirit operators supply what is necessary for the individual to see. For the more advanced students, who understand the mechanics involved, it is enough to lead them into the energy provided by Spirit and leave them in their capable hands. Spirit responds to the invitation to step closer into our field of awareness and when we acknowledge their presence the visual experience begins.

Every student questions the results of their inner seeing and blames imagination for the richness of extended sight. In time, with self-discipline and Spirit's help, we learn to distinguish between our own thought creations and Spirit ideas impressed upon the unruffled surface of our reflective mind. Until then students are discouraged from criticizing themselves or their inner seeing. Approaching their unfoldment with suspicion eventually destroys the evidence of Spirit contact they are seeking.

In earlier development groups, members sat for long periods in placid silence. Discouraging personal development, the group leader focused attention on one or two trance Mediums' development. All other members of the circle were assured of their usefulness when told they were *power houses*! Mediumship and Spiritual Unfoldment are available to every student in the methods suggested here.

After a short period group members, under the leader's direction, slowly return from their experiences. The extended consciousness can be reeled in as one would reel in a kite and the value of learning to do this shows in future unfoldment. The consciousness can always be *consciously* controlled by the individual. When beginning my development in a circle group, I made the silly mistake of thinking I had to reach a dreamy, light-headed, hypnotic state in order to see what Spirit had to show me. My kite flew to the extent of its lengthy string. Of course I achieved nothing other than a feeling of disorientation. The group leader, a very fine Medium recognized the symptoms and loudly demanded my immediate return from the extended heights I had reached. She told me to look at the Indian girl kneeling before me, which I did. Astonished by the scenes clarity, I watched a young Indian girl kneeling in the centre of a ring of Indian children. Intuitively I gathered that she was teaching them signs and symbols representing her tribal law. This experience proved very useful to me as a spiritual teacher, for I often recognize similar misunderstandings in my student's attempts to attune to Spirit.

Extended awareness is heightened awareness, but danger awaits the uncontrolled individual who insists on opening themselves to all extraneous influences. By cooperating with Spirit's directives, whether received directly or through the group leader, our awareness grows surely and steadily without undue strain upon our nervous system. In time, we need only a slight shift in our level of consciousness to be aware of a Spirit presence. But first we must recognize and understanding the need for this gear change. It is under our control when we allow this gear change to operate smoothly, quickly and naturally.

Once aware of a Spirit presence we must work at our attunement to them. By silently acknowledging, all we perceive or sense of their presence, they are further encouraged to show us more. This is a '*mind to mind*' process in need of our active participation. The person who eagerly responds to what Spirit presents, in the journey of their consciousness, meets their communicator halfway.

"Do not lay aside your precious gift of Discernment."

Janet Cyford

Chapter Thirty Four

In the Telling

Each member of the group gives an account of their experience at the end of an exercise. Moving clockwise around the group, each relates the salient points of their journey. In the telling, much more reveals itself and in time, a student learns to encapsulate the experience into brief meaning. Keeping a personal journal helps some to record details they were unable to speak of in the group time. It is unnecessary, in this instance, to open the awareness to recall and write our experiences. For, all experiences are indelibly printed upon the web of our consciousness.

One member found her beloved grandfather waiting behind the door of her choice. Another met a Spirit Guide whom he had not seen since his formative years. Although one student did not *see* anything clearly, she felt uplifted by the strong impression of the presence of a loved one, who had recently passed into Spirit.

A student experienced, an array of swirling colours that left her feeling dizzy until she silently called upon her Spirit friends for help. Their response was immediate and she felt steadied by their presence and able to complete the exercise.

The value of sharing experiences, uncovers facets of inner seeing, which only reveal themselves in the telling. There may not have been a message of guidance in the journey, there very rarely is. However, the perception has exercised itself in the safety of a well-run group and Spirit's presence.

In the early stages of development many receive, for the first time, their own evidence of a loved one's survival. A relative no longer in the physical body, projects an image of themselves, as they were when last seen on earth. Of course they no longer have a physical body, but common sense tells us, we must receive a recognizable image to know who they are. They must also think strongly of what they wish to say to us. It is important to consider that it may not be an easy process for our loved ones to achieve. By making allowances for their difficult task, we can meet them half way, appreciating and encouraging their efforts.

Exercises for personal development, in the capable hands of Spirit, expand the consciousness so it can travel through vivid scenes, created in thought by Spirit workers. It is a controlled journey of the unlimited consciousness, which is not subject to, the confines of time and space. One may walk through scenes in ancient Greece, but still be aware of sitting in one's place in "The Ring of Chairs." There is no sensation, of rushing through space to arrive at the Spirit designated scene. Although sensations may touch the physical self, it is the *released consciousness* that experiences the event.

Extended awareness, consciously controlled by the individual, can be withdrawn from its extension at will. The physical self may register some sensations as the awareness expands. Feelings of enlargement affecting the head and fingers are common, and beginners are asked not to be alarmed, when experiencing this for the first time. The sensation does not continue for many moments and is the result of one's energy registering the presence of a Spirit companion. Not all students experience this, but it is wise to prepare them, before they become alarmed by the sensation.

As our development continues, Spirit reveals deeper meaning to the images we see. In a journey instigated by Spirit, the contents are most often symbolic. Allegory and symbol can tempt us into a different type of journey, in which we research for other meanings to a symbol. Watching an eagle soar in a developing group experience, may lead us to a line of inquiry that discovers, it is a symbol for great attainment. The eagle flies very high and sees its goal in great detail. The symbol may also be a clue to a guide's name, one who joins us to teach from his own knowledge.

Each moment of group work is put to good use. To sit for long periods in unproductive silence, is not conducive to the development of mental . With time filled by structured exercises, Spirit advisers closely monitor each student's unfoldment. No time is left for idle chatting, or for the mind to wander into avenues of unrelated thought.

Chapter Thirty Five

New Groupies

When a new person joins a group, they are carefully nurtured through the first session. By keeping a close watch on their reactions to the circle format, their ability to harmonize with the existing group members, and the content of their first inner journey, the group leader assesses how they will need further guidance.

Focusing attention on a newcomer, does not detract from the other group members' progress. Quite the opposite, for as they take part in a lengthy visual exercise again, they can measure their own progress, against early experiences. The group may have moved on to more stringent exercises, but the type of inner work chosen by Spirit, is always geared to the new persons needs. Without fail, each new member experiences a first journey, which is full of meaning. Invariably, they are met by a loved one now in Spirit. For some, it is their first experience of clairvoyant sight.

A new student joined a group for Spiritual Unfoldment. In childhood he accompanied his parents to various Spiritual Healers and Mediums in different parts of the world. Having seen for himself, he had an open-minded approach to my work, disciplined by his scientific, medical training. His first session in group remains in my memory. Background sounds accompanied his imagery fitting perfectly with the tropical scenes his consciousness travelled through. As he saw exotic parrots in jungle foliage, our own parrots supplied the whistles and screeches. A large white Cockatoo and two green Amazons, had their own room in another part of our house. Usually well behaved they remained very quiet during my groups. On this occasion, with perfect timing, they supplied the appropriate noises.

At some point, each new student dismisses their experiences as imagination! Only time will tell if wishful thinking has created their inner seeing, or if it holds details, their rational mind could not have known. We have an inborn quality that investigates and categorizes information. We can at times fool others, but unless we have lost our personal integrity and discernment, it is rare for us to deliberately fool ourselves. The sensory perceptions received during this part of our group work, come from a source exterior to our everyday mind. If we lay aside the possibility of imagination creating what we want to see, we can filter and assess information through personal discernment. In a spirit of inquiry, we must wait for further proof, for constant personal criticism eventually destroys development. Spirit coworkers will do all they can to help and we need to cooperate, by using integrity to discern the source of our information. With experience, we know if what we see and hear, comes from Spirit, or from the creation of our thoughts and behaviour.

For example, the religious person will see religious symbolism when seeking spiritual understanding. The person who spends time, reading or watching horror stories, will be aware of dark images, as he or she begins to open their awareness. An attraction to, *being frightened,* cloaks their fears in unpleasant imagery. Only with personal discipline can one rise above this. The Law of Like Attracting Like, draws further unpleasant experiences to us, until we overcome this habit by seeking other entertainment.

Chapter Thirty Six

Clairvoyance, the Art of Clear Seeing

It may be of some use to all who desire Spirit contact, to discuss at length, how we expect to *see* Spirit. Many wonder why they do not appear as solidly as we see each other. Quite simply the energy required for this feat depends upon the physical make up of the onlooker. In the deceased's determination to be seen by a loved one they may gather enough material energy, from objects in the home, to enable them to appear with some substance. However, this is rare and is in part dependant upon the mediumistic qualities of the one they appear to. In certain types of circle groups sitting for the development of physical phenomena, Spirit forms can be seen by all present, irrespective of clairvoyant sight.

However, our discussion here is of Mental Mediumship, the ability to *see* clairvoyantly with our inner sight. Many proficient, practising Mediums have taken part in organized discussions on the subject of individual perception. Although all share common threads, no two sensitive's' receive mental imagery in the same way. Therefore, I can only share my own experiences here. My extreme sensitivity blends with, that of the Spirit communicator and I *feel* like them. This enables me to describe the thought pictures I perceive. The clarity of an overlaid impression, depends upon the ability of the Spirit communicator to think with positive precision. An image of how the person looked, during their life or before they passed into Spirit, indelibly prints upon the surface of my mind. Sometimes a person may have felt very overweight while still in the body, when in actual fact loved ones saw them as slim and trim. In this case confusion will occur when the Medium describes a plump figure. Every other detail will fit a certain loved one related to the client, but this is dismissed because they remembered them as having a trim figure. Again it must be remembered the Spirit contact has no physical body, so what we are seeing is a thought created picture of themselves as they were or as they thought they looked.

My prepared awareness, absorbs the projected image, with the speed of a camera shutter. Developing and describing this imprint, is then the task before me. The process demands my attention until, through persistence, I have relayed all that is necessary. This requires me *to work at it*, until my recipient acknowledges their recognition of the Spirit form being described. Herein, lies the quality of good , if what is given by Spirit is unrecognised by a sitter, the Medium must return to the Spirit communicator for further information. Dependent upon the team work of Spirit colleagues, the Medium relies upon them to find a way to deliver information that can be accepted. Undisciplined Mediumship leaves the Spirit contact unrecognised by the client, and moves on.

Occasionally, my inner sight registers the presence of a personal Spirit Guide. On the periphery of my field of awareness, they appear as a transparent, shimmering image, comparable to a holographic projection. It is essential for students, to surrender all preconceived notions, of how they will see Spirit. In this manner our Guides can, through experimentation, find the best possible way for us to work. One thing is certain, with constant use, the ability to see Spirit evolves to a state of perception that defies description. The mechanics involved, deliver evidential details of an afterlife that qualifies the Medium's gift.

We do play a part in our imaging. Spirit uses that which is in our rational mind and memory to expand and teach us. In everyday contact with others, we perceive through our personal experiences and agendas. Gaining a better concept of the various levels of our being, awakens us to the infinite possibilities, of our consciousness and the outreaches of the mind. Without this effort, we continue to function with the smallest portion of our *selves*.

Spirit blends their consciousness with ours. If our mind is filled with intelligence and a variety of interests, it holds a wider choice of vocabulary and experience for Spirit to call upon. However, if we are full of fear or religious guilt, we spoil all we receive with suspicion. An antagonistic stream of thought, created by our imagination functioning on its lowest level, always fills us with doubt. It destroys any attempt to gain further proof and confirmation. This impedes our unfoldment and it may be best in these circumstances to withdraw from this type of development.

Spirit contact requires loving cooperation. Love withers and dies in an atmosphere poisoned by criticism. If we constantly find-fault with what we perceive, our development ceases, until we can deal more honestly with ourselves. This occurs with regularity in the person whose learning may have been by rote. When presented with intangibles that defy description, this mind-set is shaken by uncertainty. Words cannot describe Spirit contact. It must be experienced for oneself and accepted according to our lights.

"It is the released consciousness that transcends the confines of the rational, critical, everyday mind."

Janet Cyford

Chapter Thirty Seven

Closing and Protecting
the Extended Energy

All that remains in a newly formed group is to carefully close the extended energy, by bringing it to a more manageable size. Group leaders and students often neglect this important aspect of personal discipline in the development circle. When working in altered states of awareness, our energy and consciousness expand considerably. The group setting enables this to happen in complete safety. Students learn to experience the extension of awareness and become proficient in their ability to reel in the extended consciousness, to a more manageable level.

Before the group closes in prayer, it is important to lead students though a method of closing the extended sensitivity. The group leader's last responsibility is the greatest one. It is her task to lead the group members gently back into the inner sanctum where their spiritual journey began. As the consciousness switches its focus away from heady experiences and embraces once again the strength within the Spiritual Self, the field of sensitivity folds as do, bird wings after flight. Closing the doors of perception brings the consciousness back to everyday alertness and we can drive home safely.

Our carefully forged links with Spirit colleagues do not sever when closing down, but remain ready to continue their guidance, through inspiration and inner prompting. However, without closing the extent of our awareness, we put ourselves at risk, by neglecting this important task of self-discipline. When these portholes remain wide open, we extend a welcome to any lower influence attracted by our light. In time, our mental, emotional and physical health suffers, due to the constant barrage of lower thought vibrations.

Eventually, the fine protective web that filters extraneous thought, weakens and we become influenced by thoughts that are not our own. An analogous example, compares our sensitivity, to the porch light constantly bombarded by every bug in the universe.

141

Beginners are also asked not to open their awareness, to the same extent, until they return to the safety of the development group setting. It is unwise to sit alone for development, once they have joined a group.

If it is the group's choice to work with Spirit, they will impress upon the leader many variations on the theme shared here. Begin each group with trust in Spirit. They will guide and enrich the work, in a manner that is suitable to every member of the group.

Chapter Thirty Eight

The Student

It is beneficial to meet a perspective student before they join a development group. This allows time to explain the nature of the group work and to tell them of certain requirements needed. It is best to determine, before accepting a new student, if they have a genuine interest in spiritual matters or, are just curious about this work. Adding a new member disturbs the existing harmony or adds to it. An upbeat personality brings a positive effect that can enliven the group energy. Whereas a someone who brings a negative, critical approach dampens the proceeding.

A student must have a commitment to persevere in their development, and enough patience to follow through, when they feel they have reached a plateau. Therefore, it must be understood, their progress depends on applying themselves to growth and unfoldment. The spiritual awakening, which comes with unfoldment, must be applied to every aspect of their daily lives. There is no set formula for Spiritual Unfoldment and Mediumistic development. Each student is individual and only Spirit Guides can decide how best to awaken these latent gifts. The circle group provides a safe environment, in which students learn a safe way to extend the consciousness and a safe way to close it again.

Carefully planned activities, orchestrated by Spirit coworkers, structure group work to the individual needs of the students. By following instructions from the group leader, personal development comes under Spirit direction. There is no guarantee a student will follow instructions, so this necessity should be fully explained before they join a group. If they cannot cooperate with the circle leader, and follow simple instructions, they will not be able to listen to and follow Spirit's directions. An explanation of the group dynamics will illustrate the need for regular attendance. Group members must have the discipline to attend regularly and not let petty excuses keep them away. Those who only attend when they feel like it, lack commitment and disrupt the smoothly run circle group.

By joining a group we make an appointment to work with Spirit friends. Each student's Spirit colleagues are ready to begin, in spite of a student's absence. An upper circle formed by our Spirit colleagues diligently prepares suitable conditions for each group session. Enthusiasm generated by Spirit workers can be felt as the group is opened in prayer. When entering this work, there is a deep commitment by Spirit to help each student in their progress. There is a far greater effort on their part, than is apparent. Irregular attendance for group work thwarts Spirit in their efforts, absent members in their individual development, and the group as a unit by greatly diminished energy.

The continuity of our unfoldment is a personal choice, and it must be a choice free from coercion. This Spiritual Law is followed to the letter by our Spirit Guides, for coercion by another is detrimental to the Soul's progression. The work of Spirit is non-denominational and a student must not abandon their chosen religion. Spirit teachings embrace all faiths. With respect for every pathway, they acknowledge that all roads lead to the one God, the Great Spirit. They do not speak of redemption through another, but teach a personal responsibility for all thought and actions that are our own. Advocating self reliance, they ask us to grow with knowledge of the Spiritual Self within.

The group member who cannot relax and would rather be somewhere else, creates a thought stream of frustration that disturbs the harmony of the group. They are told to delay their unfoldment until life creates a need for them to continue in this type of discipline.

Details of similar work done by the potential student can reveal their suitability for Mediumistic development. Along with their motive for seeking unfoldment, their goals and expectations should be clearly understood by themselves and the group leader before they are accepted as a suitable candidate for development. The student who has a modicum of psychic ability must also free their mind of previous training and cooperate with the circle leader.

The practicing psychic has difficulty fitting into a development group, for they often resent the strict adherence to Spiritual Unfoldment before message giving. This creates a challenge to the format and discipline of group work, and to the Spiritual Laws that require us to seek Soul refinement and spiritual knowledge, essential to Mediumistic development.

Some students have a personal agenda that is not apparent when first meeting them. It soon appears they expect Spirit colleagues to solve, every personal problem, by removing all that obstructs the achievement of their chosen goals. Their reasoning is working in cooperation with Spirit should exempt us from life's difficulties and they become rather heated when they find this is not so. This attitude often accompanies a high-minded sense of spiritual mission to do the work of Spirit but only in the way they see fit. Their struggle is a painful one, for their free will must be surrendered to the will of the Great Spirit, this is all that is needed. It is the ego's battle, for the intellect conceives a great plan and wants recognition for the part it will play. Within their sense of self-authority they lack humility and the patience to place themselves in the hands of Spirit and a higher purpose. The gentle approach requires too much of them. Having glimpsed the road ahead, they wish to organize every detail and despair when their efforts do not produce the results envisioned.

There may well be a prearranged Soul choice, to work with a Spirit inspired plan. The Soul, however, needs to be tried and tested to strengthen its weaknesses, and the obstacles *are* the initiation for the task ahead. Our zeal does not preclude us from Soul lessons, the harder the trial, the greater the Soul. Our ego's sense of superiority challenges the Soul's purpose. Humility is the leveller in these situations, it puts things in proportion and sets us in place again. It is wise to remember, we have only a small part to play in Spirit's plans and they do not rely upon us alone.

The talkative wordy student is a nuisance in group, and must be restrained from having too much to say. This appears mostly in the opening and closing prayer, where only one or two sentences are expected from each group member. The same personality often has a sanctimonious manner, that irritates and offends. Constant reminders are given, but all that can be said, will be said by this individual. Clairvoyantly it shows as an indentation in energy around the offender. It creates an uneven weight that spoils the continuity of Spirit light and power as it binds us together.

All group members must respect the rule of confidentiality. Personal matters revealed in this intimate work are confidential and students do not repeat these things outside the group. Spiritual snobbery needs discouraging, for it has no place in a development group, where it damages those with less confidence. Therefore, words are carefully chosen when explaining the mechanisms involved in . If a *higher vibration* suggests to a student, advancement or superiority, they have misinterpreted its meaning. True knowledge comes from personal experience and Soul growth shows in an ability to attain self mastery. Spirit asks for nothing less from us.

In an earlier group, challenges were made to the circle leader, by two individuals, whose previous experience should have taught them to know better. One admitted ignoring instructions to close the extended awareness, as they felt it unnecessary. (A dangerous habit if one needs to be alert to drive home.) Prayer will assist the process of closing down, but only personal discipline will shield the heightened sensitivity. By reeling in the extended consciousness to a manageable state, we protect ourselves on finer levels of awareness.

A lack of spirituality in the individual, who thought there was nothing more for him to learn, finally broke a group apart. Our work together had continued for sometime, when Spirit colleagues showed a division in the circle, which grew rapidly and divided the group. Disbanding the circle after the closing prayer, it reformed at a later date without the offender. A band of energy, created of dislike and disapproval, originated from one group member. It was directed towards a young man, whose inner light shone with a gentleness that only inner spiritual knowledge brings. The creator of this antagonistic stream of thought, wrongly classified the young man with long hair, as a drug addict. Long hair, according to this individual, was synonymous with drug taking.

Spirit has difficulty working in these inharmonious conditions. They are detrimental to Spiritual Unfoldment and Mediumistic development. We are taught by Spirit to put into practice what we have learned of Spiritual Law. If we see with the eyes of our Spiritual Self, it is obvious *we are all one*. In this understanding, it should naturally follow, that we cannot judge or condemn another by appearances alone. Genuine spirituality sees beyond the physical shell into the Soul of another. However, jealousy has its roots in the Soul recognition of another's spiritual qualities.

Chapter Thirty Nine

Self Mastery & the Student

Finding a sensible method to begin our development can be difficult. Without the support of like-minded companions sitting regularly with us, the task is slow and fraught with the danger of self delusion. There are no finer teachers than our Spirit Guides. If we can discipline ourselves to join a group that sits for Spiritual growth and Mediumistic development, we can begin our work with Spirit.

Be clear in your motive and purpose for wanting to develop these gifts. The Law of Attraction comes into being when we seek a teacher and a safe method in which to unfold. In thought, ask God to show you a way to find the help you need. If you wish to develop your inner sensitivity, you will without the early discipline suggested, become overly sensitive to everything around you. This can be upsetting when you are not sure whose mood you are expressing.

Seek Spirit guidance in your Spiritual quest and let their teaching help you to discover the inner life. This is the safest course and it will hasten your unfoldment. Allow them to be in charge of your development and the eventual work you do for the Great Spirit. If we have a strong desire to develop a particular aspect of Mediumship, we interfere in our unfoldment. We may be unsuitable for trance control, therefore, Spirit will work with other aspects of our nature and help us to develop the ability to be a fine Spiritual healer or clairvoyant.

When one ability comes to fruition, other aspects of Mediumship also develop. However, the individual who specializes, develops far quicker than one spread too thinly over many subjects. Your task is to forge a strong link with Spirit and to work on self- mastery. Self-discipline is the first step, for, until we can know our *self* and bring emotions and thoughts under personal rulership, we have little self-mastery.

In your personal development, act with dignity. The first sign of a true traveller on a pathway of self- discovery is their *silence*. They do not speak loudly of all they think they know, neither are they seeking fame, fortune, control nor power over others. They are quiet, gentle people who share their knowledge with those recognised as having the same understanding.

If you join a group for spiritual growth, you must respect the rule of confidentiality. Personal matters are often revealed in this intimate work and nothing must be repeated to outsiders. If we give explicit details of our development, to those with little understanding or interest, we invite ridicule and disgrace the confidence Spirit has in us.

There is a need for personal responsibility as you begin to work in cooperation with a Spirit Guide. Many students seem to think their Spirit colleague will live their lives for them. They expect Spirit Guides to give advice and make decisions on the most trifling matters. No Spirit guide of any calibre, will issue orders or opinions on matters we should be dealing with ourselves.

Relinquishing all personal responsibility for inappropriate behaviour, the student's flimsy excuses places blame on their Guide. "*My guide told me to do it*" is nonsense and to act in such a way invites ridicule. There is no overshadowing of our personality or personal willpower and if a student insists this be so, the source of their information needs questioning.

Those wishing to draw attention to themselves make constant and loud references to "*their guide*" during everyday conversation. By breaking the cardinal rule of silence in these matters we invite further ridicule. Our Spirit friends always act with dignity and we must do the same by holding our tongue. Thankfully, these students quickly lose interest in any further development, when they realize much is required of them and the path ahead is not full of material rewards.

Questionable motives will impede our further development and the cooperation of our guides and Spirit workers will disappear. An ability to make contact remains, but loss of Spirit guidance and help leaves us wide open to the influences of those who inhabit lower vibrations. The Law of Attraction draws like-minded companions to our side and our questionable motives are then supported by their company.

Ask yourself why you want to be a Medium. Can you work in cooperation with Spirit? Can you commit to the process by regularly attending your group circle? Do you wish to help others through their grief and loss or are you seduced by monetary gain and personal recognition? If your will opposes the Will of God, your efforts are soon thwarted by Spirit companions, who remove themselves from any plans for self-promotion.

The struggle to overcome the smaller self is a life-long task, and it becomes even greater for the sensitive whose has reached a certain degree of excellence. There is a great deal required of the student who embarks on a journey of self-discovery. Each must spend time on self-improvement and self-knowledge to further their unfoldment. "To thine own *Self* be true," this is the honesty that Spirit can rely on. The development of is also a life-long task; no matter how good we are we must strive to be better. If we feel we have learned all there is to know, it is time to start again from the beginning.

A Spirit guide will delay a closer contact until they can gently align themselves with the Medium's energy and speak in a clearer speech pattern. A potential guide can also delay contact until the developing Medium corrects certain bad habits that inhibit closer alignment. Alcohol dulls the senses and smoking clouds the auric energy, making close contact very unpleasant for Spirit.

A personal transformation may be needed before the outreaches of your awareness can register the presence of a Spirit guide. However, there may be a prearranged pact between two Souls to achieve some advancement for humankind. In this instance they would be drawn together to continue their work, when the one on earth reached a level of maturity. One Soul elects to be the physical vehicle for the Spirit project while the partner chooses to remain in Spirit. A possible example would be the sensitive who develops trance Mediumship. The desire to work for the benefit of others, would bring the Medium and the Spirit control together in a common bond of cooperation. Both would benefit in Soul growth and spiritual understanding.

Sadly, it is often the earthly partner who fails in their agreement. Any attempt to exploit their gift is their downfall for the Spirit companion turns away, no doubt full of sadness and compassion for the weaknesses of the companion on earth.

The ability to perceive with inner eyes, is an extension of our normal senses and is a part of the totality of our Greater Self. In most people it remains dormant until one consciously chooses to use this ability. However, there are exceptions when choice is overridden. A shock to the nervous system can forcibly open the protective doors shielding the sensitivity. There have been incidents of people finding themselves with extended sensory perception after a head injury or bad fall.

An undisciplined search for instant psychic development, also leaves the individual at the mercy of incoming stimuli. Once the doors of perception open under these circumstances, they can no longer be safely governed by the individual alone. Therefore, it is wise to approach any development with caution and plain, common sense.

In a search for personal and Spiritual Unfoldment we can become confused by the various avenues of New Age thought. It may clarify matters, if we realize, we are dealing with ancient truths that have again become fashionable. Not newly invented teachings, but the wisdom of the ancients, that unfortunately is very often adulterated to fit the needs of the New Age thinker. Thankfully, if we can find our way through the hyperbole, and bypass the fortune telling, we may discover the presence of a spirituality struggling under the weight of prediction and superstition.

Psychism must not be regarded as Mediumship. Lacking the ability to reach for a Spirit communicator the psychic remains content to touch upon the field of energy surrounding another. Hopes, desires and wishes reflect in each person's energy field, past events can be easily perceived with the extended perception of one using psychic ability. Unfortunately, what the psychic predicts for the future, is no more than, the strong wishes of the person who is receiving the reading. A sensible attitude must be used if we are not to be seduced by this mundane ability. It is impressive, by the fact, one can discern the energy of another, but it is irresponsible to lead someone to believe what they wish for, will happen irrespectively of their efforts.

To illustrate this point, an incident arose in private reading for a man whose spending habits were excessive. This habit began after a psychic told him he would be given a large sum of money. Lacking any personal responsibility, he led his life from then on believing in the prediction, which has never happened. These types of communication do not come from Spirit.

The Spiritual Law governing communication between the two realities comes into effect when the Medium reaches for a Spirit communicator. The same *Law* will extract a price if we use our ability to predict future events unwisely. An early pitfall is the extension of awareness that gives moments of precognition to the beginner. The moments of pre-knowing precognition brings, can be overwhelming and many students believe they are now able to predict the future. There is a need for encouragement to reach beyond precognition; for we are easily led astray, if we lack the motivation to seek further development. Unfortunately, some will remain at this stage, never wanting to stretch their wings further. Spirit teachers wait patiently for a renewed interest, but with great sadness, they see their earthly counterpart remaining content with so little.

To seek development to impress your friends or because it is *en vogue,* is foolish and disrespectful to Spirit. This unwise behaviour may account for the many strange ideas and practices found in today's New Age Psychic scene. Without the corresponding Soul growth and Spiritual Unfoldment, the individual soon reaches the extent of their ability. Is not for the unsteady of mind, or those wishing to draw attention to themselves. It requires self-mastery, humility and honesty. When we achieve these qualities, we are unable to fool ourselves or others.

A student can become so excited with their new found abilities they will spend every waking moment seeking communication with Spirit. Mediumship is not microwaveable! It cannot be processed within minutes. Opening doors to other levels of perception requires a strong nervous system. If we proceed with caution and self-discipline the nervous system strengthens to support our development. Without caution, fuses blow and data is lost, along with our good health and precious discerning faculties. It is our personal responsibility to be cautious in our approach and practice of this subject. Do not insist on sitting in similar groups during unfoldment, for this will emotionally drain and confuse the awareness. Personal responsibility is lacking in the student who insists on sitting for development anywhere, anytime and with anyone. They soon attract some uncomfortable physical ailments and possible damage to their nervous systems.

If a student seeks self-aggrandizement, the quality of information received in their attunement, is poor. They are unable to concentrate or complete the simplest of exercises during the development group sessions and often have a know-it-all attitude. This mind-set creates an antagonistic thought stream that eventually destroys the loving harmony of the group. In these circumstances it is best to ask the offender to leave as the welfare of all the sitters must be considered.

Difficulty following instruction from the leader of a development group, is the first clue the student has not yet reached a level of self-mastery. Inability to follow directions is not conducive to the cooperation our Spirit guide's expect from us. The student who follows their own course should definitely not be sitting for development, nor seeking any altered states of awareness.

An increase in one's sensitivity can be difficult to deal with. With practice and a sensible approach a student learns how to contain the sensitivity and protect it from overuse. Working in altered state of awareness places strain upon the nervous system so the process of development should be gradual and disciplined in order to strengthen the nervous system. Care is necessary when closing the extended field of energy after the group session. This should be obvious but accepting the importance of closing down is often a student's biggest stumbling block. Many have ignored this teaching until circumstances have proved them wrong.

When one works in an altered state of awareness, the consciousness expands. Naturally there should be a reversal of this process or the nervous system suffers. It is your *personal responsibility* to take good care of yourself with love and respect. The growing sensitivity becomes vulnerable to discord and unpleasant conditions. If we learn to shield it with Spirit's help, we can avoid the effect of situations inharmonious to our growth.

Spiritual Unfoldment brings a refinement to the auric energy that eventually permeates the physical shell. Some begin to distaste particular foods previously enjoyed and easily digested. Small differences are recognised, as the sensitivity recoils from over indulgence on the material level and we develop a need to live more lightly upon the earth. Common sense must be used or we become weird and complaining. It helps to acknowledge we live in a material reality, but the Soul and Spiritual Self are not of this vibration.

Whether our goal is to be of service to others, or to achieve inner spiritual growth, we must be aware of the danger of constantly seeking altered states of awareness. We would not leave the doors and windows of our home open to all and sundry to enter as they wished. For the same reasons, we must protect our vulnerable sensitivity, by closing all portholes of awareness until we are ready to resume our development. Serious students discipline themselves by opening these doors of awareness, only in the weekly development group. Constant use of the awakening sensitivity has a depleting effect on the health. The physical body can become a damaged vessel bearing the cracks produced by an overloaded nervous system and strained emotional self. Spreading oneself too thinly over many psychic subjects impedes any true development of one's potential.

This earlier discipline is necessary to avoid the pitfalls ahead. If the heart is free of self-promotion and the character strong, attunement is easily mastered. Inspiration and guidance received from a higher source will fulfil our desire to be a coworker, with Spirit. We must then listen to our inner voice, for Spirit speaks to us in symbols, inner prompting, hunches and feelings of certainty.

"The sign of a true traveller on a spiritual path is their Silence."

Janet Cyford

Chapter Forty

Drugs and Medication.

During a particularly trying time, I found myself in hospital, struggling to overcome a staph infection, abscessing after cancer surgery. Morphine eased the pain, but as with all narcotics, it temporarily dulled my inner sight and my ability to see my mother and other Spirit companions. Awareness of their presence was difficult, as I could not raise my consciousness to its usual level. However, through pain and fear my senses registered a most unusual sight. An angry red cloud hung at the foot of my bed. Remaining there for sometime, it grew insistent. It had a hypnotic quality and only my mother's voice, helped me to resist being drawn towards it. The strength of her command, to ignore the *Holy Joe* creating the scene, helped me see in clearer detail.

A none too healthy entity, from the lower realms of the afterlife, pushed a blood soaked robe towards my bed. Offering this as my only salvation, the scene's creator became angry when I refused to accept the robe. The religious dogma colouring the offering was overwhelming, as the entity's angry insistence continued to create the ugly red cloud.

I am grateful for the constant support that guarded me during this weakened state. Fear weakens our resolve to battle on and our ability to receive spiritual guidance; nevertheless, in all situations demanding our courage, Spirit helpers are close by to guide and support.

To those who work so hard to govern their sensitivity, the drug induced high addicts seek, is beyond our understanding. Nothing compares to, the clarity of sight and heightened awareness, safely reached when the consciousness expands . . . consciously. Once this is experienced and understood, drug induced altered states of awareness, pale in comparison.

When expansion of the consciousness is forcibly induced it is uncontrollable. An abuse of drugs or alcohol will damage and eventually wear thin the protective web shielding the awareness. This web surrounds and shields the consciousness of each human being. It is a filter that protects us from excessive noise and interference from the thoughts and feelings of others. In altered states of awareness, the protective web extends, as the consciousness expands. If this expansion is consciously controlled in cooperation with Spirit, it becomes strong and flexible.

Without the protection self discipline brings, drug or alcohol induced trips attract thought forms created from the fears, desires and fantasies of our collective minds. Thought forms created in this manner remain close to the lower levels of consciousness surrounding the earth plane, and our unrevealed fears are easily cloaked by what we attract from these realms.

Addiction, weakens the character resolve to resist extraneous influences. Addicts expose themselves to danger on levels they do not believe exist. Under the Law of Attraction, like-minded discarnate Souls link with the physical energy of the addict or alcoholic. These entities have not yet overcome their desire to drink or use drugs and by association they experience some satisfaction of their craving through one who is still in the physical body. The addict's problem is now increased twofold. Apart from feeding their habitual need they are further encouraged by the needs of those attached to their energy. The very real danger of thought possession by those still struggling to overcome their craving, is rarely considered by the addict or those who try to help them. Laws of attraction and like-mindedness would explain the addicts ever increasing addiction.

Similar dynamics are in effect when rage and anger are un-controlled by the individual who wishes to harm another. All strong thought is cumulative and attracts the same energy. This may give a better understanding of the serial killer who claims no understanding of what led them to commit their crimes. They vacate the 'self' and all personal responsibilities during the heat of passion and many other discarnate minds supply the impetus and strength to complete the deed. Blame must not be placed anywhere else than on the individual whose temperament created their state of mind. An understanding of the dangers and far reaching effects of physical, emotional and mental child abuse will, perhaps, change the way we parent in the future.

Extended Sensory Perception

Our first giant step is to accept that there is such a phenomena as *extended* sensory perception. The ability to extend the senses, is a natural function for the human mind. Examples of extended perception, range from knowing who is about to telephone us, sensing the moods of others, precognition of coming events and vivid experiences of future disasters. Some sensitives absorb strong thoughts from companions and stray thoughts from people passing by. The occasions when we know with certainty, a friend is about to telephone, come from a mind attunement that receives telepathically. This needs a certain rapport between two people to happen so frequently. Two sisters often dialed each other's number at precisely the same moment. It was only discovered after complaining that the other's telephone line was always busy! It is rare for Spirit to be involved in such mundane occurrences. Other incidents of forewarning, involve higher functioning perceptions, than our everyday rational mind. Our Spiritual Self may be the source that warns of disasters about to happen to us, or many other Souls. It would be the spark of Divinity within us that responds to an outpouring of help from the Spirit world. Spirit workers have also been instrumental in warning us of events that directly or indirectly involve us.

When natural or manmade disasters occur, support comes from Spirit as multitudes gather to lift those that perish, free from the physical body. Although powerless to prevent such disasters, there is always a great outpouring of support from Spirit to the earth plane.

Someone may, with a sense of impending doom, dream or daydream what is about to take place. If the sensitivity is untrained, they will see this type of vivid experience as prophetic. The ability to tap into other layers of reality, disconcerts the superstitious. To this mind-set, all explanations are acceptable, other than the possibility of intervention from the Spirit world.

Our sensory perception operates on a mundane level unnoticed by the less sensitive. In the development group setting, this can be experienced by pairing students together. They are to take turns sensing information from their partner. This is not mind reading or telepathy but a use of the sensory perception in its extended state. The object of the exercise is to sense one or two details of the person's character or personality. The information perceived will come via the extended perception, which attunes to the energy of a partner. It will not come from a Spirit communicator, because the awareness is not yet attuned to Spirit in this exercise.

We should conduct these experiments ethically, with moral restraint, for we are prying into another's private space, albeit with their permission. It is however, an invaluable illustration of one's ability to attune to another energy.

After the consciousness attunes to a Spirit level, the same mechanics used in extended sensory perception, registers the presence of a Spirit companion. The communicator cooperates with us, by giving full permission for *mind to mind* sharing. This method of fact finding, easily absorbs information when functioning on an elevated level. A Medium trained by Spirit, uses heightened perception to register and deliver a clear description of a Spirit presence.

Those with little or no understanding of Psychic ability, fail to consider the mechanics involved, when perception receives intimations of things unseen by others. The Medium who does not see a Spirit communicator with clear vision uses spiritual perception. The eyes have been called the windows of the Soul. They are the physical representation of our inner spiritual sight.

In the simple act of shaking hands with a stranger, two fields of energy meet and impressions are felt by both people. These impressions may register as feelings of like or dislike according to the compatibility of those involved. The next stage of perception involves a sensing that wrongly categorizes another by their appearance. If the sensitive, has cultivated Soul growth, they will instinctively understand, there are more to others than perceived with physical eyes. Once we move beyond judging by appearances, our sensing tells us far more.

To sense and perceive with inner sight, is a Soul ability that has nothing to do with the unrevealed consciousness. When the normal senses are in an altered, heightened state, they are superior to the faculties used by the everyday materialistic mind. These superior faculties may speak to us in signs and symbols in the same way the Spiritual Self does.

The Psychic's information comes from our energy field, they are not under the guidance of Spirit workers. If this were so, the information received by the Psychic would come from a Spirit communicator and contain evidence of Soul survival beyond the death of the physical body. There would be comfort for the bereaved, as evidence proved the presence of a loved one, belonging to the person receiving the message.

Those who can only work on a Psychic level, must align with a person's energy to *read* the information indelibly stamped within the aura. Unfortunately, our hopes and fears are fed to us by the Psychic, as future certainties. This form of prediction is dangerously irresponsible, as it robs another of the choice to change their future, by changing their attitude and the way they approach life.

Each of us holds the potential for many things. The blue print for our Soul's journey can be drastically altered by the Psychic's prediction, or achieved, by exercising our free will. Signposts point the way forward, but it takes courage to achieve all we came to do during this earthly life. We must never be diverted from personal goals by following the irresponsible predictions of the Psychic.

Neither can we ignore the responsibility involved with this type of psychism. It is not within Spiritual Law to interfere in another Soul's purpose. What the Soul gains along its journey may be of greater importance to its growth than the desired goal.

Our future is not carved in stone, the only certainty is, that we are *all subject to* the Law of Cause and Effect. What we sow, so shall we reap.

The choice to use one's sensory perception for prediction or fortune telling is a personal one. It is the easier road, requiring less of the sensitive. Our personal choice to use our gifts in cooperation with Spirit workers requires much more, but the rewards in Soul growth and Spiritual Unfoldment are worth every effort.

"Extended Sensory Perception is a blending of all five senses."

Janet Cyford

The Aura, a Field of Sensitivity

There is an auric energy that surrounds each form of life. Everything that holds a spark of the Great Spirit emits a vibrational frequency that can be sensed or seen clairvoyantly. Bad health reflects in murky colours, seen in our field of energy. It is a true reflection of our moods and thoughts, whether they are full of anger or goodwill. All that we *are* shows in this auric field. Our hopes, dreams and fears reveal themselves to the sensitive who attunes to another's auric energy.

The quality of the Soul, and its struggle to express the Spiritual Self, shows in our coat of many colours. Negative emotions reflect as an imbalance that will eventually impede our spiritual growth unless we use self discipline to master them. It is this energy that expands when the Medium prepares for Spirit contact. With prayer, its frequency rises to match that of the Spirit communicator and a blending of minds takes place.

The field of energy grows in size as the awareness extends. This occurs naturally as the circle group is opened with prayer. It illustrates the need for harmony for the sensitivity becomes highly charged and we feel, see and sense more deeply. Our interior listening heightens, once the auric energy extends. After this type of attunement we *must* use self-discipline to bring ourselves back to a normal state of consciousness by closing the auric field once again. It is essential we regain our alertness in order to function normally and drive home safely. The constantly extended awareness compares to a cloak flung wide open. You are unaware of all it touches until it becomes soiled with the stray thoughts and feelings of others.

In our daily interaction with each other, our energy fields blend in harmony or discord, registering subtle impressions or strong reactions. Unless the sensitive person notes a negative reaction and avoids further contact, disharmony escalates. Some people feel invaded in the energy exchange of a hug!

In Mediumship, Spirit, with our permission, steps gently, into the extended field of our energy. They use the energy centres of the body and the nervous system to make us aware of their presence. In the same manner one received impressions from a hug or handshake, one receives impressions from a Spirit communicator. The mechanics of perception are the same but for one exception. Prayer lifts the vibrational frequency of our energy to attune with Spirit. Then in a state of relaxation we can register their presence.

What was felt in the hug or handshake registers psychically and does not require an attunement with Spirit. When shaking hands with another, we feel with the nerve endings in the finger tips. The handshake originated from a need to quickly show a fellow traveller, you carried no weapons and were *open handed.* It remains a way to determine compatibility, but, is not an open invitation for us to invade another's privacy, this intrusion is psychism in its lowest form.

Coloured slides taken with Kirlian photography, have shown auric energy surrounding the subject. Pictures of a leaf removed from the parent plant, showed stages of energy depletion. Long before the leaf showed signs of discolourization its auric energy had faded.

The photographer worked with a British Spiritual Healer who allowed him to photograph her before and during a healing session. As the healer attuned herself in loving cooperation with her Healing Guides, her field of energy grew in size and intensity. Colours, vibrant with moving lights proved the presence of another force. There have been Mediums who could see the auric field and interpret the colours they found there.

My experience of seeing energy clairvoyantly is little, but there was no mistaking the black rage surrounding a young man who came to my home looking for his girlfriend. One imagines rage would show fiery red, but in this instance, his depression overshadowed his rage. Grey envelops the person fighting serious disease, for the life force becomes very depleted.

* * * * *

The public's impressions of modern Mediumship today, is that it is a party game with, which to entertain the guests. There have been social gatherings where the host expected me, as a Medium, to be the evening's entertainment.

We need to understand, the mechanisms involved in communication, then we can educate others in the simplicity of Spirit contact, and alert them to the very common pitfalls, sensitive's are prone to. Spirit coworkers, expect their earthly colleagues to take, personal responsibility for their health and apportion their energy appropriately. Our sponge-like sensitivity, easily becomes overwhelmed by the amount of Souls in Spirit, seeking a way to contact loved ones who grieve for them. The doors of extended sensory perception are easily closed with self-discipline, but, when very tired or distressed, my awareness is more vulnerable and some odd things happen.

During a kitchen clean up after dinner one evening, a Spirit voice demanded my attention, by shouting his name. Knowing it is better for Spirit to help someone in distress, I asked him to return during the next development group. In this safe environment, we could be compassionate and offer him help. Overtired, due to driving myself past normal fatigue, made me vulnerable to the strong wishes, of an impatient man in Spirit, eager to attract my attention.

People with little understanding of this work, ask why Guides do not protect us from ourselves. It is not their responsibility it is ours. We may cooperate with Spirit coworkers, but we are responsible for our self-discipline. Guides are not responsible for our actions, neither are they responsible when we ignore their advice. Sometimes, we need to be shocked, into taking better care of ourselves.

Some think a Medium should be exempt from illness and disease! We are all living in a physical body, subjected to the same deterioration as any other, we can get sick just as quickly as anyone else does. Disease gains a foothold when the various *selves* are out of alignment and we become, at variance within. Early training in a discipline that seeks inner balance and tranquillity would be beneficial. A Medium is not immune to disease, because they are doing the work of Spirit. However, the enlivening energy radiating from the Great Spirit, holds the years at bay for many Mediums. This ability to keep the *youth within alive* clearly shows in their stamina to recover from illness and disease.

"All living things are of Spirit, each holds a spark of the Divine."

Janet Cyford

Chapter Forty Three

Psychometry

Psychometry is the ability or art of divining information about people or events associated with an object. It is the ability to measure the *Soul history* of an inanimate object.

Indelibly imprinted on the energy surrounding the object to be psychometrized is a history of every thought and action associated with the item. By touching or being near, a sensitive can receive impressions from the object and access its history. Every piece of clothing or jewellery we wear retains impressions of our thoughts, feelings and mental attitude. If some of our experiences have been of an emotional nature, where fear or excitement has overwhelmed us, the trained sensitive receives intimations of these highly charged events.

Psychometry is a valuable tool for the developing Medium to use. It helps to hone the awareness, making it comfortable receiving pictorial images. The images received via the sensitivity, do not come from a Spirit companion, but originate in the energy of the article being held.

In the development circle, under the direction of the group leader, circle members psychometrize a piece of jewellery and describe impressions they receive. Through the nerve endings in the finger tips, information absorbed by the article can be accessed. Occasionally a student will receive an impression of a Spirit contact who has a strong connection to the article. At this point, it is important to realize the sensitive, is no longer psychometrizing the article. The awareness has expanded sufficiently for a Spirit communicator to make their presence known. They have stepped closer to the student's awareness by using their strong connection to the article and its present owner. In the earlier stages of development the awareness remains unruly until the student gains control. Many fine Mediums have used this method in the past to strengthen their link with Spirit. It remains a spring board for the fledgling to spread their wings.

One wonders if Mediums are aware of the mechanics involved in Psychometry. In the past, delivering the message was more important than the methods used by the Medium to contact Spirit. Today inquiring minds wish to know where their information comes from and need explanations of the mechanics involved in both realities.

The child who has to wear hand-me-downs or secondhand clothes, may sense the previous owner's energy and find this upsetting. During an earlier period in my life, I travelled daily on the London underground Tube system. As my Mediumistic development grew, it became increasingly difficult to avoid the mixed vibrations of the train seat's previous occupants. This became unbearable in times of over tiredness or stressful situations. With methods shown to me by Spirit, I know now how to shield my personal awareness and sensitivity.

Psychometry is an excellent exercise to use in the development group. The conditions of harmony and support, are conducive to each student's success with Psychometry. Collecting a few unusual objects to experiment with, varies the exercise. A student donated a small container of sand from the foot of the Great Pyramid. Before revealing its source, group members were told to share the impressions they received when holding their hands near the disguised package. Some students saw images of Pyramids and geometric shapes and the intensity of the experience surprised them.

My daughter sent me a small piece of stone from the Berlin Wall as a souvenir. Without telling of its origin, we used it for Psychometry. Several students experienced impressions of highly charged emotional conflict, along with images of Australia. This was correct, as my daughter's Australian friend had carried the souvenir.

This illustrates an important point to remember when practicing Psychometry. Whoever handles the article adds information from their own energy. Contamination of information must be avoided in the development group. If the same article passes from student to student, the disguised object must be placed in an open box. Each student takes the outer box as it passes to them and holds their hands over the article to be Psychometrised. All awakening sensitivity needs encouragement and this added security is well worth the group leader's extra effort.

One pitfall with this method is some students believe the task is to guess what the article is; this is not the objective of the exercise! The small fragment of stone from the Berlin Wall will not announce its identity as a piece of stone, but it will share its emotional memories.

Pictorial images of a symbolic content appear upon the inner sight as layers of impressions reveal themselves to the sensitive, who with patience, persists in the exercise. Students need to be encouraged to speak of feelings and emotional responses to the images they receive. Nevertheless, it is important to speak of these things as they occur. Holding on to details, in an attempt to understand and interpret meaning, interrupts the flow of information and creates mind confusion. A good rule to remember in all forms of communication is, *give what you get,* without embellishment and interpretation.

An earlier attempt to Psychometrize a friend's ring, was spoiled by an inability to relate my first impressions. The visual image received was of a young man emerging from a bathroom. A wet towel hung around his waist and water dripped from his hair. Instead of describing this, I tried to interpret the image. A sense of tragedy overlaid the scene, so I asked, did she know a young man in Spirit who had drowned. It made no sense to her until the scene was described in detail. The young man had given her the ring I held, shortly before he died in a motorbike accident.

The last memory she had of him was as he came from the shower. A towel wrapped around his middle and water dripping from his hair! Because of my lack of understanding, my rational mind interfered, trying to make sense of what I saw. Today, I wonder if the image came from the ring and its emotional content, or the young man in Spirit? There was no way to determine this until, Spirit taught me to distinguish between the light surrounding a Spirit form and the dullness of a thought image. Images from an object have the quality of a memory picture. Images, projected from the mind of Spirit have an incomparable light, depth and colour.

Buildings can also retain memory of events. Within the energy surrounding the natural fabric of stone, fibre and wood, memories of highly charged incidents remain indelibly printed. Most people have experienced the peaceful energy contained within a place of worship. A house filled with love welcomes visitors and they leave with a sense of wellbeing. The practice of *house warming* brings fresh energy into a newly acquired home, but a house poisoned with argument and violence has an unpleasant atmosphere, that is difficult to clear.

Many hauntings are the replaying of a violent act the building's fabric has absorbed. Extremes of emotion and personal suffering, record in detail and replay for the extremely sensitive Soul who happens along for a visit. There are places that retained many years of religious struggle between zealots who have killed and maimed in the name of Christianity. The highly charged energy-memory of these events is vivid and real to the sensitive person. Entrapped malevolent spirits who wish the living harm are often blamed, when in reality, the sensitive touches upon a recording of past events.

The same Spiritual Law of Attraction comes into play in so many instances. If the sensitive has a Soul memory similar to the particular event they tap into, they hold the key to the intensity of their experience. Researchers using recording instruments discovered sound waves emitting from ancient stone. Sadly, there are no details to share of their interpretation of the sounds.

Psychometry, the art of divination, can lay a foundation for the person seeking to widen their awareness of the possibilities of communication between this world and the next. As we realize the potential inherent in us all, we understand the superior faculties used in this art and appreciate the mechanics essential to good Spirit communication.

Chapter Forty Four

Past Life Regression

Spirit Guides cautioned me, to never seek information of other Soul experiences, by hypnotism or past life regression. Accepting their wishes without reservation was easy, firstly because I trusted their wisdom implicitly and secondly, because they often showed me when appropriate, glimpses of far memory. Until confronted with the damage done to ordinary folk who had experienced this practice, I had not questioned their reasons for asking me, as a Medium, to avoid any practice that tampered or interfered with my energy field. Spirit works within my extended field of sensitivity and therefore it is imperative, it is not *frequented by entities* from lower thought vibrations.

Past life regression seemed to be en vogue during the early eighties, when past life regressionists mushroomed overnight.

In true Spirit fashion my they showed me, the irreparable damage done to the auric field of energy, when the zealous amateur dabbles. Those with little knowledge of the fragile nature of our sensitivity opened doorways in their client's energy welcoming all and sundry to step inside. The dangers of undisciplined, forcible entry left the regressed-client, at the mercy of unwelcome visitors.

The premise of the regressionist's work seemed to be twofold. Firstly, that present day personality quirks, could be traced to unresolved events or idiosyncrasies of a previous personality. Secondly, the present personality is continuously bothered by entities hooked into their auric field of energy. Only by speaking to these freeloaders and sending them on their way, can the regressionist make the client well again.

However, those who had *hooked in* appeared to be children or youngsters, whom, the practitioner explained, *had lost their way* on arrival into the world of Spirit. It has been my experience that no one, especially children are left alone when they pass over. Why would a child attach itself to a stranger and create havoc? Children are not abused or disregarded in the afterlife, as they are here. All are taken into the loving arms of Spirit relatives. Whether these are relatives known in this life or another, no child is left to wander alone.

So what does this type of regression tap into? If the regressed client has anyone attached or residing in them as many believe, has the sensitivity been previously tampered with, leaving them with little mastery of their own vessel? Or are they play acting, trying to please by providing, what they think the past life regressionist requires? Another possibility must also be considered. The world of Spirit is intimately involved with our own and many pranksters have fun at our expense, by claiming to be, who they are not. This undisciplined practice carries the same dangers as *playing* with a Ouija board.

The first premise holds more water, insofar as genuine recall could reveal the roots of a neurosis as a *bleed over* from the previous personality. However, the patient's desire to create a life, richer in substance than their present one, or to excuse a lack of personal responsibility in this one, are factors to be carefully considered. The professional therapist, using an open mind, will consider all possibilities. Acknowledging the danger of misinterpretation, he is by far, the one qualified to take his patient on such a journey. As in all things, a little knowledge is a dangerous thing.

Meanwhile, for those who wish to cooperate with Spirit teachers for the sole purpose of becoming coworkers *in service,* it is crucial to their wellbeing to avoid hypnotism or regression. Those practising Mediums, unaware of the ramifications of this type of intrusion, need only look to the time in their life when preparation for Spirits work, led them to relationships where, they fought for the right to be an individual.

There is an excellent book on the subject of reincarnation and controlled regression, called Many Lifetimes, by Joan Grant and Denis Kelsey. As a psychoanalyst, he found his patients often regressed beyond birth experiences, into far memory of other life events. When he met, his soon to be wife Joan Grant, her excellent clairvoyant faculties helped to distinguish, genuine recall of past life memories, from the false intrusion of another Spirit entity, eager to tell their tale. Here lies the crux of the matter, not all regressions tap into far memory. Mostly, the story told comes from another personality with a tale to tell. Further difficulties arise when the *channel* opened during regression, cannot be closed again.

Chapter Forty Five

Spiritual Healing

There is a power, which comes from the Great Spirit, that fills each living thing. In its physical manifestation, it is the life force, within each of us. This power, called the healing energy, is available to us all. We can, if we wish, attune ourselves to it. In the silence of ourselves, we may ask the Great Spirit to replenish us with the power of healing energy. We can also place another, by name, in the stream of consciousness that holds the power. This is Absent Healing.

There are some rare individuals, who have a natural ability, to act as a conduit for the healing power and can use this gift to assist others. This is Spiritual Healing.

The healing power can be touched by anyone, but the ability to be a spiritual healer cannot be taught by an earthly teacher. Sensible methods can be shown, by those who understand the mechanics of healing energies, but the potential healer must be prepared to take instruction and guidance, from their Spirit teachers, who will demonstrate the Spiritual Laws governing this science.

The first requirement, is to work upon our own nature and practice self-discipline. The healing gift develops, if one has a strong desire to be of service to others, by lessening pain and suffering. With compassion, sympathy and a desire to alleviate another's suffering, we can attune ourselves, to the stream of consciousness that holds the power to heal. It is a very rare form of Mediumship, for the spiritual healer, must be free of strong ego and the desire for self-promotion. They have also achieved a degree of self-mastery. Where there is a natural Mediumistic ability to heal, attunement and cooperation with Spirit come easily. Strong and willing bonds, forge links between the healer and their coworkers in Spirit. Through a long friendship and familiarity with one's Spirit counterpart, a prearranged goal to work together, may have been chosen, before the earthly healer incarnated.

Very often, this is only understood, within the deeper levels of the healer's consciousness. They are content to simply lay their hands on another, in a sincere effort to bring relief from pain and suffering. Through experience, they know of the help they offer others. Where there is a natural gift, a detailed explanation of the mechanics used in the healing process, is not required by the healer, as they know its ultimate source.

A state of wholeness can be regained, with the help of Spiritual Healing. The various bodies that make up our total Self, must come into alignment with the Spiritual Self, before the balance of good health returns. Spiritual Healing, can assist our recovery, but it must not be viewed as a substitute for medical attention. It works together with, and not against, your physician's advice.

Disease is a condition of imbalance, often caused by being at variance within ourselves. Our thoughts and emotional reactions to life events, can create an over emphasises within the emotional or mental self. Extreme, prolonged anger, envy, or fear accumulates within the corresponding self and creates a protrusion that will eventually tip the scales of balance. The resulting tension, seeps through to every aspect of our being. If we can govern our thoughts and emotions, not letting them rule, we can maintain an equilibrium that always supports us.

Times of emotional or mental stress are often followed by a feverish head cold or virus, from which it is difficult to recover. The physical self has an intelligence of its own and can warn us, through inner prompting, to take better care of ourselves. We need to remember our physical body is the vehicle, the indwelling Soul and Spiritual Self, uses during its earth plane experience.

Once we elect to do the work of Spirit, we begin the never ending task, of seeking self-knowledge, to enable us to be a reliable instrument.

The process is one of team work between a group of Healing Guides, Spirit operators and the earthly healer. A healer is often aware of a change in energy, as a different Spirit worker joins their group. Some do not possess inner clairvoyant sight, but can however, register the presence of different Healing Guides working within the healing power.

Degrees of effectiveness are due to the various Spirit workers, who may specialize in areas of healing. Their choice, comes from a long association with the healing arts, much as our earth doctors choose to specialize, in a particular field of medicine. The healer in Spirit, is subject to the Law of Attraction, which draws them to work with healing power, corresponding to their Soul's progression. Those of us with clairvoyant sight, are often aware of Spirit healers and teachers swathed in colours depicting their spiritual attainment.

Spiritual Healing, along with other spiritual gifts, can become distorted with complicated practices, and strange types of behaviour. Some believe the energy used, is drawn from the earth, or from other living things. Several exponents use their own energy to heal, however, this practice, eventually drains the healer and the recipient, of their energy.

Spirit operators do not need the personal energy of the healer, for they use the healing power that comes from God. Directed through the earthly healer, the vibrational flow is adjusted to the needs of the person seeking healing. The desire, to be a Spiritual Healer, must carry an awareness of the responsibility involved. Without dignity, integrity and humility, the healer's need for personal drama and adoration, will eventually destroy their ability to heal.

Spirit colleagues, always act with dignity and we must do the same. Many potential partnerships, between this world and the next, have been spoiled in the early stages by our lack of self-discipline. The Spirit Guide will wait patiently for an improvement in their earthly companion's behaviour, before allowing the work to continue.

Once we put personal expectations to one side, we become clearer vessels for the healing energies to flow through us. If there is a close cooperation between the two levels of existence, Spirit and matter, the patient will benefit from the healing session. We must not allow personal desires to supersede those of the Spirit helpers.

Beware of the healer who claims to cure all ills. Promises to cure, do not fall within the Spiritual Laws governing Spiritual Healing. No one, regardless of their spiritual gifts, may interfere in the Soul growth and progression of another. The healing gift is to assist and strengthen another's will to recover.

"Each of us can attune to the Divine Healing Power."

Janet Cyford

Chapter Forty Six

Spiritual Healers

In 1955, members of my family joined the National Federation of Spiritual Healers, a non-denominational healing organization for spiritual healers in Great Britain. Membership today, stands at seven thousand and is only given to those who, acknowledge the existence of God as the source of the healing power. Until his death in 1975, Harry Edwards, a well-known and highly respected healer in the Spiritualist Movement, led public demonstrations of Spiritual Healing with the NFSH. My mother, father and aunt, took part as healers in many of these public demonstrations. Each National Federation healer, wore a freshly laundered, white coat with the blue and gold, Federation logo on the breast pocket. They made an impressive sight, when seen in great numbers.

To accommodate the Welsh Male Choir, hundreds of NFSH healers and great numbers of people seeking Spiritual Healing, public events had to be held in the largest Town Halls available. Once a year a Healer's Day Service was held at the Royal Festival Hall on the south bank of the river Thames. Organizing these affairs required team work by willing Souls, who, one expects, received recognition and acknowledgment when they arrived in the next world. So often, good work is overlooked and unappreciated, among the inflated egos, large organisations produce or attract.

Members of the NFSH are bound, by a strict code of conduct, in order to keep the practice of Spiritual Healing, dignified and orderly. My aunt, often spoke of an experience, however, which angered many healers who witnessed it. In the changing room, a woman pulled on her white coat in preparation for the healing service. Then, with a noisy display that attracted attention, she began to dance and spin around. Disgusted by the spectacle, my aunt asked her why she did this. The lady explained that, although she did not enjoy this ritual, her guides required it of her. In fact, she added, they were unable to use her for healing, unless she did as they asked.

My aunt assured her, this was a figment of her own imagination. No self-respecting Spirit coworker, would expect their earthly partner to act in such an undignified way. The fault lay in the woman's need for drama and display. Each of us must eradicate these habits and stupid practices if they are part of our personality. There is nothing more disturbing, than to see this wonderful work, reduced to vaudeville. It should be a point of personal discipline to always act with dignity when demonstrating the work of Spirit.

In 1959 Harry Edwards published a small booklet written by him, called "The Hands of a Healer" It was for private circulation among the National Federation Healers. His purpose in writing this was to remove some of the stupid practices that had grown through ignorant imitation of unnecessary techniques and healing practices. His words are as pertinent today as they were when written thirty years ago. Every potential healer should study his work and be guided by his suggestions.

Today, within the various organisations, that use Spiritual Healing in Great Britain, the practice of touching a patient during a healing session, is discouraged. These rules were formed in an attempt to prevent any unwanted familiarity by the healer. Physically touching the patient to direct healing energy is unnecessary. To hold the outstretched hands, within the auric field of energy surrounding the body, is sufficient.

My own early experiences of Spiritual Healing, quickly taught me to listen and obey instructions, from a Spirit guide. Following directions to attune myself to Spirit in silence, my awareness soon registered the presence of a new Spirit companion. He instructed me to reach in prayer to the Godhead and when ready, to step closer to the patient's chair. During healing services at a Spiritualist Church, healers stand behind a chair placed for patients to sit on. My new instructor reminded me, not to touch the patient, but to hold my hands, close to either side of her head.

The healer's alignment to Spirit, is essential for the healing power to flow, unimpeded by the healer's thoughts or expectations.

Following these instructions was easy and I stood for a few moments, within the patient's auric field, with my hands either side, but not touching her head. It is a remarkable sensation, to stand within the stream of consciousness, called the healing power. Once experienced, it can never be mistaken for, or likened to, any other healing method.

Suddenly, my new Spirit companion, told me to, "Step back, the healing has taken place." I ignored his directions three times, believing them to be of my imagination, until dizziness and depletion forced me to step out of the patient's field of energy.

With very little reflection, I realised, my reluctance to move, came from fear. Fear of the patient's reaction to this simple healing session, that had lasted only a short time. No sweeping passes were made. Neither did I shake my hands to free myself of the patient's energy. A habit adopted by many who believe energy attaches itself to the healer and must be shaken free. It is a ridiculous notion with no purpose, reason or meaning. Unfortunately, it is a habit copied by healers internationally. Feelings of pins and needles in the hands, are not uncommon, when the healing power passes through the energy centres in the palms.

Feeling embarrassed and uncomfortable over my performance, for there was nothing to show for the time spent with this patient, I quietly told her the healing was finished. Fulfilling my worst fears, she loudly complained, "Was that all there is" and her sharp comments added to my discomfort. However, the memory remained, reminding me of the pitfalls our ego can lead us into. Impressing the patient, far outweighed my need to trust and follow my healing guide's instructions.

The composition and tone of healing energies are adjusted for each patient. The process, achieved by Spirit operators, who understand the patient's needs, happens rapidly. An outpouring of healing power may flow through the healer's energy centres, solar plexus and hands. The healer's energy is not used in this process. The quality of our Soul, taints or flavours the healing power, but Spirit has no need to use our personal energy.

Unless the healer recognises the divine source of healing power, and attunes to the source, their own energy is rapidly depleted. Ignorant of the mechanics of Spiritual Healing, they unconsciously draw upon the patient's life force. This results in both patient and healer feeling worse for the experience. Some New Age methods of healing use physical energies, not realizing this is unnecessary. Attuning to and taking direction from, our Healing Guides, prevents these silly mistakes. Only cooperation develops a method of directing the healing power. In step with their instructions, the earthly healer becomes a finely attuned instrument for Spirit's work.

My mother, Irene, had a gift for Spiritual Healing and an ability to receive Spirit diagnosis. This was always gently passed onto the patient, with encouragement to seek medical attention. She had a wonderfully strong link with Spirit, but no medical training. This type of communication, received during a healing session, carries a responsibility for the healer, who must not give medical advice. It is the patient's responsibility, to seek medical attention, if Spirit diagnosis suggests the need for this.

Spiritual Healing is not a substitute for medical attention, but a valuable addition that speeds the patient's recovery, on many levels of their being. It is a recognised therapy within the National Health Service in Great Britain. When asked, doctors can refer patients for healing and NFSH healers, are allowed to give healing to in-patients, who request Spiritual Healing. It is officially listed and openly received and therefore, has no need to be disguised as Therapeutic Touch.

My mother firmly believed, healing energies are enhanced, by the minds of doctors, who have passed into the Spirit world. Choosing to work with their earthly colleagues, like-minded Souls, gather to inspire new advancements in medicine and surgery.

She plays an important role in my work for Spirit, and her early transition at fifty seven, did not end our companionship with each other. I am constantly aware, of her participation, during my group work, seminars and private consultations. Her presence enriches my own work and her gift for getting to the root of a problem still comes into play.

Chapter Forty Seven

Spiritual Unfoldment.

We may seek Spiritual Unfoldment, through the development of Mediumship, to enable us to better navigate our chosen pathway. There are many ways to do the work of Spirit. Care-givers who join a group, develop an inner strength that helps them to withstand the pressures of dealing with the terminally ill. Our knowledge of the Spirit world's reality and a surety of the continuation of life can support others, for we carry our spiritual link into everything we do. The raising of consciousness we have attained through our Spiritual Unfoldment, draws other like-minded people to us by Soul recognition. If we allow our new found gifts of the Spirit, to make a difference to our lives, the light from our inner Spiritual Self shines through.

The development of Mediumship must be accompanied by the corresponding Soul culture and Spiritual Unfoldment. When we recognize and integrate all levels of our being, the Greater Self blossoms. It is a transformation, which reveals us to be a spiritual being, inhabiting for an allotted time, a dense physical body. Soul culture manifests when we overcome the limitations of the present personality and seek access to our Soul's knowledge, experience and wisdom.

The sacred journey, to become whole within and at one with God, only begins when the consciousness turns away from the concerns of the outer personality. Our spiritual quest must lead us within, to search for the unrevealed Spiritual Self. This aspect of our being is not unconscious of its nature or the accompanying Soul's plans for further evolvement. It patiently awaits recognition by the present personality, who prefers to look for self-realization in the material reality.

It is the conscious, rational mind of the personality that remains unconscious of its imprisoned splendour. This continues until circumstances contrive to awaken the personality to its source of strength within. Our life takes on new meaning once we recognize the inner strength at our disposal.

The Soul can be illuminated by the Divine light of the Spirit within. But it remains a glowing ember until fanned by the Soul's efforts to be an expression of the Spiritual Self's Divinity. This is the aspect of our being which responds when we turn inwardly to seek Spiritual Unfoldment. It is the ability to switch the focus of our consciousness beyond the rational mind that eventually releases the imprisoned splendour and stirs the indwelling Spiritual Self into manifestation.

Spiritual Unfoldment, requires a purification of the outer earthly personality and its penchant for warring elements, which elude and confuse self-identity. The purification demands we work to overcome the smaller self with discipline and self-mastery. There must be resolve to tame and educate all aspects of the present personality, so that it yields and concedes to the Greater Self and the Soul's pathway.

Owning personal responsibility for all our thoughts and actions, brings the realization that our present circumstances, are the results of our creations. We do, in fact, word and deed create our own reality. When the great Spiritual Law of Cause and Effect is acknowledged, we embrace life and allow the Spiritual Self to guide and direct our future pathway. Individuality and spiritual gifts the Soul has earned, need to be nurtured and cultivated, for, it is the creative expression of these gifts that support the Soul's evolvement. Unfoldment shows in those who refuse to see their present conditions as reward or punishment, but as opportunities for the Soul to seek direct experience. They understand the Soul's journey weaves through peaks and valleys as it strives to achieve at-one-ment with the Great Spirit.

Self-awareness allows us to observe our reactions so that we learn to *Know the Self* in all circumstances. Remember when judging or condemning yourself or another, we are travelling a road that is mandatory to each Soul's progression. When the consciousness comes into the presence of the Divinity within, there is no condemnation or harsh judgement but total acceptance of our strengths and weaknesses.

With unconditional love, this spark of the Divine gives us strength and courage to try again. Our Soul gains support for its efforts, to learn quickly and thoroughly that, which it has drawn to its 'self' to experience.

Balancing the emotions with self-mastery is a difficult, but necessary task. Without stability the emotions continue to swing from one extreme to another and cannot be relied upon to support us in our work for Spirit. But when balanced and tempered with reason, each emotion adds support to our Soul growth. Poised and serene, our disciplined emotions can be relied upon to not run amok in times of stress. Thus, enabling us to function placidly from the very centre of our being.

In the development of Mediumship it is essential to overcome the extremes our emotions can subject us to. This is not to imply that our emotions need suppressing, for that is detrimental to our well being, but rather, to suggest they are properly governed. Observing emotional reaction to situations reveals personal patterns that build or destroy our character. We build an emotional self, fashioned from our emotional reactions. It can be fluid and flexible, or rigid and constricting, depending upon the present personality's stronghold and the Soul's evolvement. It is this layer of our being that determines our physical and mental health and which also impedes our Spiritual Unfoldment through its unalignment.

Uncontrolled, unreasonable fear stems from a lack of trust in an all-knowing and all-seeing spiritual power. Fearing loss of personal control and will-power suggests a lack of understanding of the strict Spiritual Laws our Spirit Guides are subject to. All that is required of us when seeking Spiritual Unfoldment is loving cooperation. We have freedom of choice at all times and none are overpowered by Spirit for this is not within Spiritual Law.

Sympathy and compassion are wonderful spiritual gifts, but our sensitivity must be governed from identifying to the point of absorption. Unless well-regulated with personal discipline, another's suffering and sadness eventually affects the Medium's peace of mind. Jealousy and criticism destroy love and are emotions that are detrimental to Spirit's work.

Greed is a negative state of mind that cannot thrive in the light of the Spiritual Self. It should not be allowed to reign. Emotions, balanced by personal restraint and a watchful eye, stop the negative thoughts from interfering in our development. We are progressing in our Spiritual Unfoldment when the emotional self supports us in all we do. With restraint, it no longer responds in anger and irritation to those things that are a vexation to the spirit within.

As an emotional self is formed of our rigid or flexible emotional reactions, so a mental self is created from our thinking patterns.

With the same self-discipline our thoughts must be tamed in all manner of ways. We create our own reality, with our present thoughts we create that, which is in our future. If we repeatedly tell ourselves that something we fear is so, we create and draw to us circumstances that prove our fears to be true. By changing our thoughts we change our future.

An example of this truism, is the reality created by our collective thoughts, concerning the death of the material body. The golden years of old age are blighted with fear of the unknown, when a different approach would have one preparing for the wonderful reunion ahead. Strength to pass easily through this porthole comes from within at the time of each Soul's transition. The damage to our peace of mind that ingrained, unreasonable, rigid beliefs do, are immeasurable. By overcoming the present personality, the *individuality* seeks to experience the tenets of life and death for itself. It is not content to accept the written word as true, nor the spoken word as the final interpretation. Facts and figures, polls and statistics do not account for unknown factors and the inquiring mind, aware of the vast potential of the consciousness, quests for its own answers.

We must watch our thoughts carefully, so we can determine the source of their creation. Ambiguous as this may sound, it is in thought that all Spirit communication takes place. With constant monitoring, we can recognize where our information comes from. If a Spirit companion has triggered a sudden thought or whether this has arisen from some deeper part of our consciousness, can only be recognised with practice. A third possibility comes from our very humanness to think by association of ideas.

My personal experience is that my mind is constantly chattering, taking part in an inner dialogue that is self-perpetuating. Without realizing what I was searching for, I repeatedly rewound my thoughts to discover their beginnings. I found that many mundane inner conversations began with an association of ideas. The following example may illustrate this more clearly.

While preparing potatoes for dinner one day, I suddenly found myself thinking of Geraldine, a Medium who once stayed for the weekend in my home in England. My mind wandered through memories of this delightful lady. I was convinced she was thinking of me at that moment and I had received her thoughts. However, by rewinding the pattern of my thinking I discovered they came by an association of ideas. During her visit with me many years before, she had helped prepare dinner by offering to peel potatoes. She insisted on using a knife, rather than a vegetable peeler and had reduced the potatoes to the size of marbles, cutting thick layers of skin and vegetable from each one. By association of ideas my mind uncovered memories of her. I often peeled potatoes, but on this occasion having mislaid my peeler, I reached for a knife to prepare my vegetables and made the same mess of them as she had done a long time ago.

This method of retracing my thoughts had important ramifications. Not only did I learn to distinguish between my own thoughts and those of my Spirit companions, I found the ability useful in my Mediumship when I needed to rewind the threads of a Spirit communication. In the process of mind to mind connection, thought often arrives too quickly and consequently becomes jumbled.

There is a need to surrender our preconceived ideas of spirituality before seeking unfoldment. It is the hardest task to lay aside all we think we know and allow ourselves direct experience of the spirituality found in the company of the Spiritual Self. This can best be achieved by getting out of our own way. Experience cannot be claimed, simply because we have read many books on the subject of spirituality.

Our awakening does not begin with the intellect, or the rational mind; although both will dissect and dismiss as imagination that, which the inner self knows to be true. Spiritual Unfoldment comes, not in sudden flashes of religious ecstasy, but in a new found approach to the difficulties in our life and a new joy in our experiences. When all aspects of our various selves balance in perfect alignment, the core of strength within stands tall throughout our being and we are truly functioning from the indwelling Divinity.

Spurts of inner growth, if not assimilated slowly, bring us to a plateau, where we could become discouraged with our progress. Until we can surrender, embrace and unconditionally accept what is occurring within, we can reach no further. By first seeking self-knowledge, we reach an understanding of our human nature and the need for self-mastery. A sensible approach will guide us cautiously, with common sense, through any method of Spiritual Unfoldment and Mediumistic development. Self-control is a quality, essential to our safety and welfare. It is a discipline that needs cultivation before our work for Spirit begins.

Chapter Forty Eight

The Power of the Spirit

Every living thing holds a spark of the Great Spirit. Knowledge of this great truth was paramount for native people, on all continents across the world. Recognizing the Spirit within nature, they lived close to the earth and treated all living things with respect. Mother nature supported mankind's welfare and he took from her, with gratitude and reverence for the gift of life. Today, our preoccupation with materialism, greed and acquisition has clouded our remembrance of the nature of the Great Spirit and we have lost *respect*.

By disregarding the Spirit in all living things, we as a human race, have fettered ourselves with a retribution that will be difficult to overcome. Disrespect for the Divinity within all God's creatures, does not diminish, but merely dims our spiritual light. Its power remains unused until such times that events in our life, compel the present personality to defer to the indwelling Soul and remember the meaning of respect.

Great spiritual teachers have come to the earthplane to explain this truth, expressing their knowledge by the very manner in which they lived their lives. Very few have understood them, for the Spiritual Laws they taught and lived by, were too simple to accept. When interpreted through the narrow eyes of intellectualism, simple truth becomes inaccessible by distortion. In this confusion human beings relinquish personal responsibility, refusing to think or reason for themselves.

Neglecting our connection to the Great Spirit, we are subject to religious interpretation that further encourages us not to question our own Divinity. We allow ourselves to believe, we can only know God, through the intervention of another. One who, to boot, has taken it upon themselves, to guard the way. For many years, a great outpouring of spiritual power has bathed the earthplane. Its purpose, is to bring human beings to an awareness of their own creations, and the need for personal responsibility for what has been created. The perfect Law of Cause and Effect balances the ledger of life. It is time to acknowledge our accountability.

We need to raise our consciousness to understand the spiritual truths that have been too simple for us to accept in the past. Our spiritual progression as homo-sapiens will continue to stagnate, until all respond to the spiritual energy now embracing the earth. We must begin by, knowing the *Self*. With this knowledge we can find our way into the inner sanctum of the Divinity that is the light of the Soul. This is where all answers can be found.

When we believe, Divinity is beyond our reach or comprehension, we feel at the mercy of a judgmental deity who allows dreadful things to happen to us. Some say they do not believe there is a higher power. By not reasoning for ourselves, we give credence to a definition that is limiting. We choose to ignore our inherent Divinity, believing we have no personal power. It is easier to blame a personified deity for our problems, and difficult to believe, human beings, not God, are personally responsible for the evil in this world.

As a human race, we cannot prevent these things from happening, until we allow our Spiritual Self to manifest. It can then direct our lives into avenues of higher thought. Matters will remain the same until we all function from a Soul level and express the Divinity within. There comes a time in every life when one is forced to seek an inner strength to rely upon. We relinquish our personal will when we can surrender to the *Will of God.* In this simple realization an inner power rises to support us and self reliance is born. It is an unfortunate reality that we wait until we are overwhelmed and despairing before seeking the comfort of Divine strength.

How simple it would be if we were encouraged, from an early age, to seek God's presence in the inner silence of ourselves. Finding a method to experience our Divinity would uncover a spirituality that constantly guides us. A lack of self esteem disappears when an individual experiences the dormant, imprisoned splendour.

With an awareness of our true nature we think before setting in motion events, that eventually destroy the peace of mind and wellbeing of others. The Great Spirit gave children into our care, to protect with love and teach by our example. They do not belong to us, but to the Spirit within. When taught respect for themselves and others, each child grows in fertile ground knowing they have come from God, and that they hold a spark of the Divine nature.

To experience the power of the Great Spirit we must create a silence on an inner level. If we allow the focus of our consciousness to withdraw from the material life, it will journey inwardly into the presence of the Spiritual Self. Here, a tranquillity and serenity are found that is beyond description. Once we recognize our inherent Divinity, we begin to experience its power in our growing confidence and new attitude. Then, by making room for its presence, a spiritual pathway reveals itself.

A holier than thou, sanctimonious attitude, will not smooth the pathway. Neither will spirituality develop at the expense of others, for we are of the same Spirit, irrespective of our colour, creed and gender. The individual who gains Soul growth in their lifetime is mindful of their speech and actions towards others.

This material experience will continue to be a difficult one, until our growth reflects in expressions of kindness in thought, word, and deed. Our physical self is the temple of the Soul and Spirit and a deeper understanding reveals the Soul's connection to the Great Spirit. We finally understand the thread that joins us as one when we give credence to the fact that we are all journeying back to God.

Today there is an urgent cry for help as we watch our world diminished by greed and disrespect for the life force. We disregard those who know the life of the Spirit and try by example to show the way. These special Souls, share their knowledge despite ridicule. Opposing forces, created by the egos of the self-serving, seek to disgrace them and diminish their efforts. Until the power of the Great Spirit takes its rightful place in our lives, humankind's tremendous potential will continue to function poorly with greed and disrespect.

The power of our thoughts can achieve great things, if influenced by the wisdom of Spirit and the experience of the indwelling Soul. When we hear of a friend's struggle with illness or addiction, we must discipline our thoughts away from the cause and effect. Ask the Great Spirit for strength and courage to support them in their battle with the 'self.' Surround them with healing filled with vibrations of wellbeing. In so doing, a strong link forges with Spirit and support comes to them from those who elect to work with us here on earth.

Our thoughts create the type of leadership we are under. If we are a nation of people filled with materialistic greed we will find this greed expressed through those we elect to rule us. Being intent on achieving wealth at the expense of others, we create the very conditions of poverty we are trying to avoid. Unfortunately our creations come to fulfilment in a later generation and cause greater problems of resentment and hardship. To eliminate greed and selfishness in those in authority, surround them with the light of the Great Spirit, for this will reveal all that wishes to remain hidden in darkness.

In the reality beyond our own, we come to a deeper understanding of the Great Spirit. Through the eyes of the Soul we clearly see that created by Spirit and that which is created through our materialistic greed. We create our own reality here on earth. However, the full implications of our creations are only apparent when we pass into the world of Spirit.

In thought we create the conditions around us and then blame God if our life is not all we want it to be. Our thoughts and actions attract into our environment, acquaintances who add joy or despair to our lives. Through Soul recognition, the Law of Attraction draws like-minded companions to us. While in a physical body, we can hide our thoughts and emotions. However, we are not exempt from the law of *like attracting like* for it is always in effect. Our future, moulded from past and present thought and actions, changes as our motives improve. A change of attitude towards all aspects of our existence will alter our lives. Relying upon the spiritual power within, we can amend, what we have set in motion with our thoughts and actions.

This process requires patience, as there is often a great deal to rectify. We must stop blaming others for our behaviour and take responsibility for our own actions. Then a different journey begins, one the Great Spirit will oversee. If the desire to change is genuine, many workers in Spirit smooth the path to recovery. In contrast to our own creations, the Great Spirit's mind builds with the power of unconditional love and the beauty of compassion.

When we pass into the next reality, we can no longer mask all that we are with the physical shell. This vehicle was shed by natural process at the moment of death. Without this shield our thoughts, feelings, emotions and motives clearly show for all to see. An environment, compatible with our past thought and actions, awaits us in the next reality. Not fashioned by a vengeful deity, but created by us.

Many face death with an overwhelming fear of the unknown, but if our Soul can supersede what the rational mind fears, the consciousness is easily released from the physical self. The Soul's existence is eternal, it has *been*, it *is*, and it *will always be*. Therefore, it is the Soul's recollection of its immortality that assists the *separation of consciousness*, death of the physical body brings. So much mental turmoil could be avoided if inner attunement was encouraged from an early age.

A wonderful reunion with those that have gone before awaits us as the consciousness finds clarity in the afterlife. The threads of love begun in our earthly life are not severed by death, but continue to bind us together. It is our expectations that enable us to see them waiting to greet us. Our loved ones are there despite our mind-set, but our rigid thinking can build a barrier to our awareness of them. In these instances the consciousness remains in its own creation, until it seeks of its own volition, a deeper understanding. It soon tires of its own restrictions and longs for a lightness of being.

Where there is strict adherence to religious teachings, some Souls program their consciousness to wait for Gabriel to sound his trumpet, summoning the dead to arise. Some believe that death is a revolving door, where one lays *in state* awaiting the next incarnation. This rigid state of mind must soften to become aware of the wonderful Souls waiting patiently for them to reawaken. No one is left alone in these circumstances, they are watched over and surrounded with the light of understanding. However, they must respond to this light of their own accord, fulfilling their personal free will.

Some firmly believe Christ will meet them at the time of their death. The intensity of his light is beyond anything we can imagine and would overwhelm the Soul in its transition. The Christ consciousness holds a peace available to us all, but, in this particular expectation God's ambassadors would minister to the new arrival.

No one is left comfortless. All are taken into the loving arms of Spirit workers who choose to be with those who feel alone. Some individuals remember how to die. They demand of the Greater Self, do not let me suffer! It is not a plea for mercy, but a command to be released from the confines of the physical body.

Chapter Forty Nine

Creativity

Through our connection to the Godhead, we manifest the Spiritual Self through creativity. Allowing this spark of Divinity to take its rightful place in our lives, we can, if we wish, touch upon levels of thought that transcend the lower materialistic mind.

Each Soul must free itself from the constrictions of the worldly self and book learned knowledge. Then our consciousness can reach to a level of thought compatible with our Soul's progression. In this attraction we can tap a vast pool of knowledge past, present and future. It is a meeting of minds in the Law of Attraction.

An ability to be a specialist in a chosen field of creativity may come from many lifetimes that may not have been without sacrifice. The Soul has a burning desire to express what it knows of Spirit, for knowledge shared benefits others. Hampered by the confines of the physical self, the Soul seeks to express its spirituality, in creativity.

Creativity is every child's gift and imagination its playground. Each Soul brings, experiences gained and gifts acquired, into a newly fashioned physical self. Lucky is the child whose parents appreciate its gifts. Sensible parents, do not stifle a child's creativity and imagination, but provide fertile ground for the child's uniqueness and Soul growth.

Parents accuse children of telling tales if they speak of imaginary friends only they can see and hear. These playmates are Spirit companions children have the innate ability to see. Childhood is close to the world of Spirit, only the ability to tell of its closeness is missing. Clairvoyance, the ability a child uses to see Spirit playmates, is a natural gift in childhood. However, children will close the doors of perception when they feel ridiculed and misunderstood. Teaching a child to distrust this ability begins a deterioration of inner seeing and reliance upon the greater 'Self'. By sowing a seed of doubt and allowing it to grow, the ability to see Spirit is lost and for some, never regained. From then onwards the child will ignore the inner prompting of the Spiritual Self and live a colourless life.

Yet, if these sensitive traits are recognised and appreciated they will flourish. Adults should encourage and positively reinforce each child's imagination. Our imagination is part of the creative force and is integral to our inner harmony. It is an inherent capacity of the mind that allows the Spiritual Self to speak to us in symbol and imagery.

Unfortunately, many people still hold the archaic opinion that all imagination is fanciful day dreaming. If this opinion takes-root in a child's awakening sensitivity, they mature mistrusting their imagination and its inspiration. Consequently, a lack of self esteem blocks the future development of natural creative expression.

Mediumship, the ability to communicate with the Spirit world, is a cultivated gift of the indwelling Spiritual Self. It is a mystical art form originating from the same creative energy that inspires all artistic endeavours. Spirit communication is possible through the cooperation of many Spirit minds. The Medium's ability is the vehicle for its expression.

By the same Spiritual Law of Cooperation, when an artist acts upon a creative thought, the source of all inspiration responds with the same Spirit cooperation. In the artist's attunement, inspiration comes from great artistic minds of the past, whose creative capabilities remain within a collective pool of consciousness.

Musicians speak of music they first hear on an interior level. Writers tell of clear thoughts that are their inspiration. Along threads forged in sensitivity, rapport establishes our connection to the source of all inspiration. Creativity, the power and ability to invent, is the vehicle for our imagination. We create our own reality here on earth with our thoughts and opinions. The same law applies in the world of Spirit.

Nurture gifts of the Spirit into full expression. They atrophy if disregarded, as a limb will wither and die through lack of use. Our creativity can be a balm to the Soul or an irritant if frustrated by lack of opportunity to express itself. The highly evolved Soul lacks competitiveness. Neither is it judgmental nor self conscious. These destructive qualities are taught by example and encouraged by those who stand in authority. When each child is given a safe and secure atmosphere in which to grow, the indwelling Soul expresses its presence with ease.

Respecting a child's inner life allows the spiritual essence to become the guiding influence. Conditions are then ripe for creativity to unfold and the Soul progresses, hand in hand, with the Divinity, the God within.

If, individuality is encouraged and uniqueness respected, we have few psychological problems to overcome. Our sense of self-worth is apparent in self respect and the respect we give to all living things. We have joy for the accomplishments of others and choose good role models to emulate.

Good physical health reflects the health of the inner life and our willingness to accept the indwelling Soul and Spiritual Self. Bad health, may have its roots in an emotionally crippling childhood that crushes the ability to be creative. Thus building a structure within the emotional self that twists and binds us into an unnatural state. Emotional crippling creates an imbalance that disturbs the natural alignment of the various selves.

We must find a way back to the source of creativity to regain our balance. A healthy inner life allows us to deal with our pathway creatively, for we have reliance upon an inner strength that never deserts us. When our inner voice directs the heart, head and feet will follow. If the personality allows it, the Spiritual Self can stand tall, erect and powerful. Then we can access a source of strength and all-knowing, our inner splendour, the kingdom of heaven within.

"Learn to live more lightly upon the earth.
Requiring less and giving more."

Janet Cyford

Chapter Fifty

The Prayerful Life

There is no exception to the validity of personal prayer. It is the key to the expansion of our awareness, for prayer naturally changes our vibrational frequency. To enable our inner sensing to unfold we must raise our vibrational rate. Once our consciousness is raised, we experience the natural function of spiritual sight and Soul sensing. Prayer focuses our thoughts.

Many voices uniting in the words of a familiar prayer create a field of energy that can be seen by Spirit. It extends outwardly from the place in which the collective prayer is spoken.

Composed of the lightness of thought, the prayer energy rises to a level of like-minded thought. This accumulation reaches its goal through the impetus of desire, motivated by the person or persons praying. As the spoken prayer rises from the earth plane it is a wonderful sight when seen through the eyes of Spirit. Rich in colour, our prayerful thoughts hold a personal pattern, an individuality that is unique.

Thoughts are living things, as we think, so we are. If the thoughts and desires, which mingle with our prayers are for the betterment of humankind, or to uplift the downcast, we draw to ourselves conditions conducive to our own growth. To live in the energy of prayer is to have joy and enthusiasm for life, irrespective of the circumstances we find ourselves in. Prayerfulness is a state of mind that responds to the spirituality within each living thing. It is not a matter of spending many hours on ones knees in prayer, nor is it built from perfect attendance in church. Neither can it be reached through prayers learned by rote. It is only created through unconditional love and acceptance of others' strengths and frailties.

195

Prayerfulness is a natural state for the Spiritual Self to be in, for the Divinity within us, knows the hand of God is in all things. When we allow this inner splendour to direct our life, it generates an optimism that is infectious, and life is lived with a sense of wonderment, acceptance and openness to a vast array of experiences. Prayer fosters an inborn trust in a power that helps us navigate our pathway and fully embrace life.

A natural state of prayerfulness can be found in the child who is loved and accepted for its uniqueness. The child looks for the best in all things and shows an inner assuredness that is every Soul's birthright.

By our adult actions we teach our children to doubt themselves, carefully discouraging them not to rely upon their perceptions. In the early years of each child's life the closeness of Spirit is unencumbered by the rational mind. The Soul holds fresh, clear memories of its Spirit life, until unpleasant physical experiences supersede the inner knowledge.

Our society focuses on the development of intellect and ignores the indwelling Soul's intelligence. We carefully teach our offspring fear and encourage competitiveness, with no consideration for the real need for individuality. The crippling effects of child abuse mark the physical and emotional self. This far reaching damage inhibits the expression of the indwelling Soul and hampers the emergence of the spiritual essence. Unless the Soul is strong enough to overcome the adverse effects of abuse, the life will be lived at half-measure. Joy for life is paralyzed and our natural ability to lead a prayerful life is denied.

Examples of the Soul's strength show in those who do survive such harsh, barren and hostile beginnings. The inner strength struggles to support the balance of mind, by reminding it that this too, will pass. If the Soul reigns, it surpasses the physical, mental and emotional fettering of earlier abuse.

Chapter Fifty One

Symbology

The Spiritual Self speaks to us in symbols. In an effort, to remind us of our Soul's need for creative expression, symbols ancient and universal, rise to the stilled surface of the mind. They are a link between Spirit and matter. We ignore this rich source of information until we seek a spiritual pathway of development. A search for symbolic meaning leads us into avenues of thought unrealised by the rational mind.

Freedom from dogmatic religious interpretation allows a universal expression of Spirit. America's Founding Fathers were well acquainted with ancient symbolism and its deeply spiritual meanings. They relied on Divine guidance to lead them, knowing this would come from the Divinity within. Many Great Souls came together at a time in history to share their knowledge for the birth of a free nation. Indian tribes, gave inspiration for the division of power. A symbol of spiritually elevated consciousness, was chosen in the Eagle.

The same symbol appears in astrology. The sign of Scorpio has three symbols, a Scorpion, an Eagle and the phoenix. It is the natural eighth house of the Zodiac, ruling the creative life force and transformation. A Scorpion's poison can kill. People with the sun in Scorpio, who function on a mundane level, battle to overcome problems caused by procreative energy. Those who raise the same energy through the body's energy centres, transmute the life force into spiritual understanding and become the Eagle, a messenger of the Great Spirit.

The phoenix is another aspect of transformation, for it rises from the ashes and begins again. Ancient symbols are found in heraldry, the coat of arms used for royalty and ancient European families.

Symbolism disguises meaning that is inappropriate to the esoteric shopper. They are easily identified by their scattered knowledge of a great many subjects. Without seeking spiritual unfoldment along with their psychic development, they lack the dedication to master one avenue of attunement.

America's one dollar bill is rich in Masonic and Rosicrucian symbolism, and reflects the ageless wisdom understood by those who founded the nation. In ages past, only initiates were allowed access to ancient knowledge. Mystery schools throughout history required evidence of self discipline and self control before the candidate was accepted for initiation into the mysteries. The oath they vowed reminded each candidate of their personal responsibility to respect sacred knowledge by using it wisely. They were sworn to secrecy to protect all wisdom from misuse by those who cannot recognize its sacred value.

Students sitting for the development of Mediumship and spiritual unfoldment sit in a circle formed by a Ring of Chairs. A circle is a universal geometric shape that creates a natural flow of energy. Moving in a clockwise direction, each student adds one or two sentences to the opening and closing prayer. This left to right movement synchronizes with the upward spiral of energy Spirit operators use. The opposite, right to left circular movement, is conducive to lower occult energies. The complete circle drawn with a central point, symbolizes the Divinity within each human being. It is the symbol for, God incarnate in humankind.

In this symbol the circle represents our outer personality and material life. We cannot leave the circle's circumference, so remain in a continuing cycle of similar experiences. From every position on the outer rim there is a different perspective of the central point in the circle. This point seems inaccessible until we find a way to enlarge the centre. By letting it expand the centre becomes the circle. When humankind functions from their inner essence they have a vastly improved point of view.

Number and alphabet contain circles, straight lines and semicircles. The perpendicular line represents the upright, honourable person who deals, with all living things, in an upright, honourable way. A perpendicular line when crossed by a horizontal line becomes, the cross of crucifixion. Symbolically, the horizontal line represents our humanness, frailties, and imperfections which are to be overcome. Crucifixion of the lower self on the cross of matter, allows the upright honourable person to gain knowledge of the Greater Self. This attainment reveals the true nature of, Spirit incarnate in man.

Ancient knowledge, retold in parable and legend kept great spiritual truths alive from generation to generation. To preserve spiritual teachings, knowledge and wisdom was recorded pictorially. The spiritually mature learned to decipher each pictorial symbol according to their Souls' progression. However, the uninitiated used these images for card games and fortune telling.

Three meaningful symbols pass unnoticed by the materially minded Souls among us. An insignia, modeled on Hermes' staff is the emblem used by the medical profession. The caduceus, a winged staff with two entwined serpents, was carried by Hermes as the herald's wand. Two entwined serpents represent the life force in two aspects, masculine and feminine. Entwined they climb the staff or spinal column. Another name for this messenger of the Gods is Mercury. With winged feet, Mercury spreads news with the speed of thought.

Combined, these two symbols of winged thought and the life force, hold deeply symbolic meaning. Spirit teaches that mind is the builder, individual thoughts are living things that create our reality. The way we think effects the physical body's life force and our health expresses our thinking patterns.

The two glyphs, symbolizing Venus and Mars, used in medicine, represent male and female. This symbolism is self evident but further meaning reveals itself when studying the lines and circles used. A circle, placed above the cross of matter, is the glyph for Venus. It is the Egyptian Ankh of life everlasting. This comes when we build a relationship with the inner self, the Divinity within. It is the union of the outer personality and inner individuality, gained by creating harmony and balance within.

The glyph for Mars is the reverse of Venus. A cross of the material world now sits above the circle of Spirit. A cross, now representing our ability to procreate, is elevated by the Spirit within. The person who fought and won the war with the lower 'self' gains self mastery of the life force on its most potent level. He or she is liberated by understanding, that it is our disrespect for the procreative life force, which leads to dis-ease.

A spiritualization of the Mars energy, when raised through the body's energy centres, brings an alignment of human will, with the will of God. When the creative force stimulates the higher centre's, our ability to perceive with an inner sight will function effectively. Raising our consciousness to function above the belt activates the energy centres used for communication with the world of Spirit. Herein lies reason for caution in our esoteric search for psychic ability. Without the corresponding soul culture and spiritual unfoldment needed in our safe development, we put ourselves at risk of being overpowered by our lower nature.

Examples of this downfall can be found in those leaders who have not gained a measure of discipline of their earthly appetites. Being subject to the power of office can corrupt the best of us. Prayers for strength and courage should be part of each persons daily life if they wish to seek high office. And an understanding of our very human nature should be reason enough for us to pray for our world leaders.

We see energy, power and control, expressed in the world today, through war. The longest war, being the battle between the sexes. When using the energy and action of Mars with compassion and respect for all life forms, we become a spiritual warrior, not the warlord. The Mars energy needs constant self discipline if raised through the centres of energy. Carefully monitoring our thoughts, prevents strong energy, rebounding through the centres. For this very reason, our psychic and mediumistic development must be under the guidance of Spirit, in the safety of a well-run group.

Fairy tale and myth speaks to us in allegory and symbolic meaning. Mars and its symbolism, appears as the hero, facing a difficult scary journey, which can only be travelled alone. This journey stands between him and a lifetime of happiness. In ancient tales, the hero took the magic sword given by the old wise man, who represents one who has conquered the Mars energy. The hero uses the magic sword for protection as he journeys into the depths of the unknown.

The magic sword can be relied upon. For it has passed through the hottest fires to emerge as, perfectly balanced will power. As the tale unfolds it becomes evident the journey within the depths of Hades is to recover buried treasure. The hero must slay many dragons barring his way, before the final battle with his 'self' is won. In more modern myths the hero learns to align and attune with the force within. He relies upon intuitive perception, rather than that seen with his physical eyes.

Tales of spiritual warriorship, found in all journeys back to God, are illustrations of the Soul's struggle to remember its Divinity. Deeper meaning unfolds in the hero's battle to temper the will of the procreative force before it rules him. The masculine force will stabilize with support, from the feminine instinct. It is she, who warns the hero of the unseen dangers ahead.

Here is a journey dependent on cooperation, with a final reward of union. A union between the masculine and feminine aspects of all life. Another interpretation needs personal experience before the rational mind can fully understand its symbolism. For the greatest 'union of marriage' is between the Soul and the Divinity within. This alchemy turns lead into gold.

Symbols speak to us, according to our Soul development and spiritual understanding. A love of symbology is the mystic's path. To study symbolism complements Spirit's training, it develops the mind and strengthens the Medium's attunement to the Great Spirit. Mythology, mysticism and symbology are the royal roads to Spiritual Unfoldment. Their study is highly recommended for the potential Medium or anyone seeking a deeper understanding of the nature of God.

When delivering a Spirit communication, some Mediums use a shorthand symbolism developed in cooperation with their Spirit coworkers. Others receive complicated imagery that conveys deeper meaning. This method enables Spirit to cloak intimate details recognised by the recipient, but not understood by the Medium. Good Mediumship does not interpret meaning, but relays information as received from Spirit. In a public demonstration of clairvoyance, Spirit prevents the Medium from revealing personal details the audience should not hear. Critics complain of hearing complicated trivia, but, if the message has meaning for the recipient, then the Medium has delivered it correctly.

Sometime before my first visit to America, I was curious to often see, a clairvoyant image of Abraham Lincoln. Neatly framed, it clearly showed his face, portrait style. Liberation from slavery was my first thought and this fitted nicely into the message given to a young man in the audience. The same image reappeared in other Spirit communications, with different meanings. Freedom and liberty from spiritual enslavement were prominent themes. The need to escape from a tyrannical, overbearing person, was another.

To be who you are, irrespective of condemnation or judgment from others is a human right. It demands personal responsibility and the need to stand upon ones own feet, for symbolically the feet are our under standing!

A rich source of symbolic meaning can be found in vivid dreams. Personal experience has shown, these to be encounters the consciousness has with Spirit teachers, guides and loved ones no longer living. The everyday rational mind, sometimes recalls a dream in symbolic form. We must be aware of this in order to interpret our visions as symbols that have deep and sometimes prophetic meaning.

My dreams suddenly took on a very American flavour, although I had no plans then to visit the U.S.A. In the light of these remembered events, I now realize Spirit was preparing me for my road ahead, but it was not apparent to me then.

One very clear dream was of Paul Revere. My children explained who he was and how he warned others, *the British are coming*. Whomever prepared me for change had a delightful sense of humour. In another sleep experience a Gregory Peck lookalike gave me his car. Parked outside my parent's old home in London, I dreamt I was sitting on the left side of the car behind the steering wheel. A car represents the body, the physical vehicle and in my dream I was given an American car by an American dreamboat.

These details passed unappreciated by me for sometime. However, they were clearly recalled and understood later. At that time I was learning to drive on the wrong side of the road, sitting on the wrong side of the car . . . newly married to my American husband . . . and living in the U.S.A.

The End

Index

205

Medium

Mediumship

207

211

Recommended Reading

Mediumship

The New Mediumship . . . by Grace Cooke.
The White Eagle Publishing Trust, New Lands, Liss, Hampshire, Great Britain
A Guide for the Development of Mediumship . . . by Harry Edwards.
The Harry Edwards Spiritual Healing Sanctuary, Burrows Lea, Shere, Surrey.
GU5 9QG U.K. Telephone (01483) 202054.
Voices in the Dark . . . by Leslie Flint. ISBN 0 85384 075 X
Inevitable Journey . . . by Donald Galloway. ISBN 0 584 10145 7

Spiritual Healing:

The Gift of Healing. . . by Ambrose & Olga Worral
Explore your Psychic World . . . by Ambrose & Olga Worral
Miracles in the Making . . . by Ambrose & Olga Worral
Journey to Awareness . . . Jane Uhlig
Born to Heal . . . by Paul Miller   (a biography of Harry Edwards)
Harry Edwards the Healer . . . by Paul Miller
The Science of Spirit Healing . . . by Harry Edwards
A Guide to Spirit Healing . . . by Harry Edwards
The Way of Spirit Healing . . . by Harry Edwards
The Healing Intelligence . . . by Harry Edwards
A Guide to the Understanding & Practice of Spiritual Healing . . .
                                    by Harry Edwards
The Harry Edwards Spiritual Healing Sanctuary, Burrows Lea, Shere, Surrey.
GU5 9QG U.K. Telephone (01483) 202054.

Spiritualism:

The History of Spiritualism . . . by Sir Arthur Conan Doyle
The University Of Spiritualism . . . by Harry Boddington.
On the Edge of the Etheric . . . Arthur Findley

Spirituality

The Path of the Soul . . . White Eagle.
The White Eagle Publishing Trust, New Lands, Liss, Hampshire, Great Britain
Spiritual Unfoldment 1 & 11 . . . White Eagle.
The Gentle Brother . . . White Eagle
Prayer in the New Age . . . White Eagle
Teachings of Silver Birch . . . Edited by A.W. Austen
Silver Birch Anthology . . . Edited by William Naylor
In Tune With The Infinite . . . Ralph Waldo Trine. Thorsons/HarperCollins.

Accounts of Life in Spirit

The Blue Island . . . W.T.Stead (Died on the Titanic)
Health Research P.O. Box 850
Pomeroy,WA 99347
Life in Spirit . . . By Harry Edwards
The Harry Edwards Spiritual Healing Sanctuary, Burrows Lea, Shere, Surrey.
GU5 9QG U.K. Telephone (01483) 202054.
Testimony of Light . . . By Helen Greaves
The Challenging Light . . . By Helen Greaves
Publishers. Neville Spearman Ltd. Saffron Waldon, Essex Great Britain
The Return of Arthur Conan Doyle . . . by Ivan Cooke. The White Eagle
Publishing Trust, New Lands, Liss, Hampshire, Great Britain

Websites of Interest

The Spiritual Healer On-Line	www.harryedwards.org.uk/
Spiritualist National Union	www.snu.org.uk/snu.htm
Psychic News	www.snu.org.uk/index2.htm
The Noah's Ark Society	www.noahsark.clara.net
Spirit Books	www.cadvision.com/spiritbk/index.html
Medium's Directory	http://members.xoom.com/margaretjohn/ indexpenpals.html
Janet Cyford	www.HomeCircles.com
Regency Press	www.buckland.co.uk/regency/

Organizations

The College of Psychic Studies.   6 Queensberry Place, London SW7 2EB
Telephone: 0171 589 3292

The Spiritualist Nation Union.   Redwoods, Stansted Hall, Stansted, Essex
CM24 8UD
Telephone: 01279 816363

The Spiritualist Association   33 Belgrave Square, London, SW1.
of Great Britain.

National Federation of   Old Manor Farm Studio, Church Street,
Spiritual Healers.   Sunbury-on-Thames, Middlesex, United
Kingdom, TW16 6RG UK
www.nfsh.org.uk/introduction.html- -
Email: office@nfsh.org.uk

Greater World Christian
Spiritualist Church.   http://user.super.net.uk/~gemble/intro.htm

Psychic News/Psychic Press   Clock Cottage, Stansted Hall, Stansted,
Essex CM24 8UD
Telephone: 01279 817050
Email pn@snu.org.uk